Career Education in the Academic Classroom

Edited by
GARTH L. MANGUM, JAMES W. BECKER,
GARN COOMBS, AND PATRICIA MARSHALL

Olympus Publishing Company Salt Lake City, Utah

ISBN: 0-913420-58-1

This work was developed under a
grant from the U.S. Office of Education,
Department of Health, Education and
Welfare. However, the content does not
necessarily reflect the position or policy
of that agency, and no official U.S.
government endorsement should
be inferred.

 **Contents**

1
Introduction to Career Education in the Academic Classroom

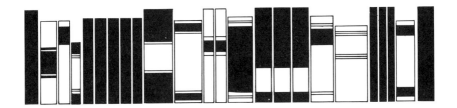

By the Editors

Garth L. Mangum
University of Utah
Salt Lake City, Utah

James W. Becker
Foundation for Improvement of Education

Garn Coombs
Brigham Young University
Provo, Utah

Patricia Marshall
Olympus Publishing Company
Salt Lake City, Utah

1
Career Education in the Academic Classroom

"Every classroom teacher in every course at every level should emphasize the career implications of the substantive content taught." One of the key components of career education, this statement was made by Kenneth Hoyt and his co-authors in various books which have helped to develop the concept of career education into a workable tool for the nation's schools. Every teacher in the school is vital to the achievement and the objectives of career education. The teacher of academic subjects — mathematics, science, English, social studies, fine arts, foreign language, physical education, and others — is as much a career education teacher as is the teacher of the practical arts and vocational education.

This does not mean that career education expects teachers to subordinate the objectives of their disciplines to those of career education. The primary responsibility of the mathematics teacher is to teach mathematics. The same is true for teachers of English, science, and all other academic subjects.

Career education offers as much as it asks. It asks teachers to pursue as a first priority the effective teaching of their subject matter. But it also asks that teachers contribute to the long-term career success of their students in ways that are not destructive of good teaching or good learning in each subject. Career education offers something in return for the teacher's help in furthering career goals. It motivates students to more effective learning by demonstrating to the student that subject matter is closely related to deeply held personal goals.

The purposes of career education are the same as the purposes of all education: to prepare the student to understand the society and the self in relation to the society, and to develop the necessary skills to function successfully and with satisfaction in that society. However, career education limits its focus to one function of self and society — that which relates to work and the satisfactions of work. The goal is well expressed in one of career education's many definitions.

> Career education is the total effort of public education and the community to help all individuals become familiar with the values of a work-oriented society, to integrate these values into their personal value systems, and to implement these values into their lives in such a way that work becomes possible, meaningful, and satisfying to each individual.

Career education's goals and objectives in no way conflict with those of the various academic disciplines, which contribute to education's broader goals by focusing on those aspects of self and society that relate to their own subject matter. Career education is not a separate course or system, but is an emphasis within all courses. It encompasses each of the academic disciplines insofar as they relate to functional uses in work. It does not restrict the teaching of these disciplines to work relevance and leaves teachers unbound wherever their own internal goals relate to culture, citizenship, personal welfare, or abstract truth outside the work context.

However, career education should not be viewed as a narrow concept, and there is nothing antihumanistic, illiberal, or anti-intellectual about it. It offers a way in which academic studies become not only important in themselves but part of the entire enduring fabric of people's everyday lives.

A career is more than a job or even a vocation. It is the totality of what one accomplishes in a lifetime of efforts — whether paid or unpaid — to provide goods and services for the benefit of oneself and others. Career education, then, is all of that education which makes available the values, attitudes, knowledge, and skills needed to choose, prepare for, and pursue a successful career throughout life. This calls for far more than job skills. It requires a complex and lengthy set of prerequisites: good mental and physical health, human relations skills, a commitment to honest effort as the preferable source of income, a willingness to accept the discipline of the workplace, and the motivation to achieve in a work setting. Career success entails all of the basic skills of communication and computation, familiarity with the tools and ideas of science and technology, and sufficient knowledge of the workings of the economy and the labor market to make possible appropriate career choices. Obviously, familiarity with all of the standard academic subjects, plus in-depth knowledge of some of these subjects, is essential.

But few students at any age will avidly pursue learning in any subject unless they see its relationships, direct or indirect, to their own deeply held values and objectives. For some, an objective may be the intensive satisfaction in mastery of knowledge or the development of personal talents. Some may take it on faith that subject matter of otherwise vague significance will somehow ultimately be relevant to their long-range goals, such as meeting college entrance requirements. Others may demand evidence that what is taught is truly relevant to them.

If students and teachers are to find satisfaction and worth in their relationships, the students must be motivated to learn in many different ways. Highlighting the career implications of subject matter will not interest every student, nor is it the only way to get students absorbed in academic study. But it will motivate many, and no teacher is wise to neglect its motivating power.

The academic teacher is not of course the only actor on the career education scene. In the world outside the school there are many others who have important roles in the career development process. Hoyt and his coauthors have identified five basic components of career education through which individuals move during their lives.

The home and family is the first school and the first faculty, and it is there that most children and youth develop their beginning values and attitudes toward work. Later, influences outside the home can make important contributions to the learning and development process. As the individual seeks to understand self in terms of values, interests, abilities, accomplishments, career alternatives, and educational and skill prerequisites, there is an enlarging role for others.

There is the classroom in which learning of academic subjects can be linked to broad career applications to motivate learning and to enable students to see some relationships between their studies and possible future careers for themselves.

There is the acquisition of productive job skills in the classroom, on a job, or in other kinds of experience. In the school setting, the courses in which skills are learned are not only those generally described in the curriculum as vocational education. Music is vocational training for the prospective musician; art is vocational training for the artist; and mathematics readies the engineer.

Next, Hoyt and his coauthors point to the role of various career development programs that expose individuals to occupational alternatives and work ethics and values, and help them to visualize themselves in different occupations and to make well-informed career decisions.

A fifth component of career education is interaction among schools, business and industry, labor organizations, and individuals in varied occupations to provide and enrich the learning that takes place in the schoolroom.

This means that to be effective career education must link home, school, and institutions of the working world into a mutually reinforcing network that forms a comprehensive learning environment.

But career education is not limited to those years of schooling in which academic subjects are emphasized. It is a process which takes place, whether by design or by chance, from birth throughout the active years of life. Schools can participate during those years when people pass through their nets — in early childhood education where it exists; in parent effectiveness training for an intergenerational impact; in elementary and secondary education; and in post-secondary, higher, and adult education for those who choose to travel these routes. But because elementary schools, junior and senior high schools, and institutions of higher education are the sources of most academic instruction, it is in these sectors that much career education must be concentrated, although not confined.

In the development of the career education idea, numerous admonitory works have been published. One series in particular, published by Olympus Publishing Company, has emphasized the practical elements with such books as: *Career Education: What It Is and How to Do It*; *Career Education and the Elementary School Teacher*; *Career Education in the Middle/Junior High School*; and the forthcoming *Career Education for the High School*. However, it is all very well for educational theorists, administrators, counselors, economists, policymakers, and others to admonish teachers of academic subjects to emphasize the career implications of substantive content in their studies, but none of these persons can speak authoritatively on the possibilities, problems, and methods involved in doing so.

On the classroom level, career education activities are numerous, primarily in the fugitive, unpublished literature exchanged among practitioners. Missing, however, has been a concerted effort by academic classroom teachers to explore the consistencies and inconsistencies between the goals and objectives of their disciplines and those of career education. For that, teachers of the appropriate academic background and educational experience must develop and promulgate the curriculum and technique. This book begins to remedy this lack.

In December 1974, the National Foundation for the Improvement of Education — a nonprofit corporation created by the National Education Association, using funds provided to Oklahoma State University from the U.S. Office of Education — convened a working conference on Career Education for the Academic Classroom. The conference was held at the Adult Education Center of the University of Maryland. Of the national associations representing classroom teachers in the various academic subjects, seven participated:

American Alliance for Health, Physical Education, and Recreation

American Council on the Teaching of Foreign Languages

National Art Education Association

National Council for the Social Studies

National Council of Teachers of English

National Council of Teachers of Mathematics

National Science Teachers Association

In addition, the National Recreation and Park Association later supplied valuable information for the recreation section of chapter 8 on health, physical education, and recreation in career education.

For the career education conference, each national association chose a five-person team that was led, with one exception, by the association's staff director and supported by four experienced classroom teachers. Each participant was given a variety of books and offered U.S. Office of Education issuances on career education, which they were urged to study carefully in advance. The seven teams then were assembled simultaneously for a three-day working conference during which they were asked to provide for their association a statement encompassing these elements:

(1) The generally accepted pedagogy of their discipline

(2) The educational goals of their discipline

(3) The relationship between those goals and the goals of career education, including conflicts or inconsistencies

(4) Important issues in each discipline which might affect its relationship to career education

(5) A description of techniques for incorporating career education into classroom activities

(6) Examples of activities useful for incorporating career education without compromising priority goals of the disciplines

This book is the product of that conference. We editors were the staff of that conference, but the content is the contribution of the teams. Their productivity, imagination, and breadth of experience were outstanding. Substantial editing was necessary, because of the pressure of time and the diversity of styles, but the contents — philosphy, concepts, instructional strategies, examples, and most of the words — are those of the participants. The edited material was resubmitted for their approval. None was authorized to bind an association in endorsement of this content, and the book was not submitted to the official governing bodies of the associations. But in every case, the chapters represent the considered judgment of a team consisting of a staff officer and carefully chosen teacher representatives from members of that association. The material on each discipline does not always confine itself to the borders of that discipline. For example, the sections on health and recreation might be read with profit by all teachers. They can do much to expand career awareness and exploration in these fields because there often are not special classes available in such subjects at the secondary level.

The Foundation for the Improvement of Education was represented by Executive Director James W. Becker and Deputy Director Dr. Margaret J. Jones, but the positions taken do not necessarily represent those of the Foundation. Olympus Publishing Company provided at its own expense most of the conference staffing and logistics and all of the transcribing, copy editing, printing, and publishing costs. Oklahoma State University and the U.S. Office of Education supported the conference but not the publication. Everyone involved assumes personal rather than institutional responsibility, with justifiable pride for individual contributions. But the worth of the effort must be determined by the extent that each chapter proves useful by:

(1) Motivating teachers across the land in that discipline to undertake career education as part of their classroom techniques and content.

(2) Illustrating for them "how to do it." If appropriately done, teachers will be able to add an emphasis on career implications without watering down course content or violating their priority assignment to teach the disciplinary subject matter. They will be able to give a greater depth of career knowledge to their students and receive in return the stimulation of a more eager and highly motivated student body.

Career education does not begin or end in the academic classroom, but it does reach its maximum significance there.

Selected References

Begle, Elsie P.; *et al. Career Education: An Annotated Bibliography for Teachers and Curriculum Developers.* Palo Alto, California: American Institutes for Research. January 1973.

Career Directions Program. Four units. Washington, D.C.: Changing Times Education Service.

Combs, Janet; and Cooley, W. W. "Dropouts: In High School and after School." *American Educational Research Journal* (October 1970), vol. 18, no. 1.

Dunn, James A.; *et al. Career Education: A Curriculum Design and Instructional Objectives Catalog.* Palo Alto, California: American Institutes for Research. April 1973.

Evans, Rupert N.; *et al. Career Education in the Middle/-Junior High School.* Salt Lake City: Olympus Publishing Company. 1973.

Goldhammer, Keith; and Taylor, R. *Career Education: Perspective and Promise.* Columbus, Ohio: Charles E. Merrill Books, Inc. 1972.

Hoyt, Kenneth B.; *et al. Career Education: What It Is and How to Do It.* Second edition. Salt Lake City: Olympus Publishing Company. 1974.

_____; and Hebeler, Jean R. *Career Education for Gifted and Talented Students.* Salt Lake City: Olympus Publishing Company. 1974.

Maryland State Department of Education. *Career Education Resource Notebook.* Baltimore: Maryland State Department of Education. 1974.

Olympus Research Corporation. *Career Education: A Handbook for Implementation.* Washington, D.C.: U.S. Government Printing Office. February 1972.

2
Career
Education
in Science:
A New Partnership

National Science Teachers Association

Robert L. Silver
Executive Director

John M. Akey
Mitchell High School
Colorado Springs, Colorado

Charles J. LaRue, Jr.
Montgomery County Public Schools
Rockville, Maryland

Fred D. Johnson
Shelby County Board of Education
Memphis, Tennessee

Margaret Nicholson
Lafayette, California

2
Career Education
in the Science Classroom

In the 1950s and '60s, one response to the demonstration that the Soviet Union could follow us into the world of nuclear weaponry and precede us into space exploration was a call for rapid increases in the production of scientists. The competitive edge previously enjoyed in science and technology by the United States seemed to have slipped precariously, challenging our ability to survive as a major political power in the world.

In the search for something to blame for this embarrassment, the schools became not only the scapegoat but also the center where change could be made most rapidly and effectively. No incentives were needed to stimulate the production of scientific manpower other than the expression of national need and evidence of available jobs in science. It then remained for the schools, and particularly teachers of science, to review the content, methods, and processes of their studies to determine where and what changes were needed.

The federal government supplied the funding for change by injecting huge amounts of capital through the National Science Foundation into the development of new curricula and to retrain and update science teachers. The new curricula and teacher retraining accomplished the goal — to produce more students who would choose a science career. The chief appeal in the new curricula was to the most academically oriented students because the curricula were theoretical in approach and almost disdained any practical application. One outcome of such an approach may have been the neglect of specific needs and interests of a large number of school youth. To the extent that these students were neglected — and they now are adults — they are likely to have a lesser degree of appreciation for science and lack the functional capabilities they should have in this field as citizens and as workers.

Historically, the science teacher's career emphasis has been almost exclusively aimed toward two areas — careers in pure science and careers in which these sciences play a major part. For example, in careers that draw heavily upon pure science — medicine, nursing, allied health occupations, agronomy, agriculture, and the like — teachers have long made students aware of the linkages between what they teach and career goals. The career focus for these students has been present not only in course content, but also in library research assignments, in field trips to see scientists at work, in visits from guest speakers who stimulate high school youth with information and insights about their work, and to a lesser degree, through on-the-job training for a few high school students.

Most chemists, biologists, physicists, astronomers, oceanographers, and other members of the scientific community began their pursuit of adult careers in the high school classroom. In this environment, they learned to adopt an attitude of inquiry, to manipulate the tools of their trade, to use its terminology, to perform scientific experiments, and to get their first glimmering of scientific problem-solving techniques. It was their first penetrating insight into the life of the scientist.

There still is a need to prepare future scientists and engineers. The importance of progress in these disciplines is well established. Science teachers must continue to expose students to science careers as a way of life and to help students with problems of career selection. Teachers must continue to describe the nature of scientific careers and to make students aware of the rewards, the responsibilities, and the steps to be followed if they want to become scientists.

But the 1970s have brought some new goals to science education. Today, the teacher must do more to open up the world of science to all students. One reason for this is the fact that society's needs have increased for scientific technicians. In order to motivate a larger segment of the student population to pursue careers in science and in science-related fields, the teacher must find ways to make the study of science relevant to these students' interests and needs. More students might choose health careers, for example, if they were made more aware of the immense range of occupations in the health field. But health is not the only science or science-related field with wide occupational options. The various science disciplines offer a host of opportunities for nonscientists in the marketing and distribution of products and in various administrative and supportive jobs.

In today's science instruction, the teacher must explore activities and instructional methodologies designed to meet the needs of greater numbers of students than have been attracted to science and science-related careers in the past. Far too many students who could make outstanding contributions in these areas have not been guided or encouraged by teachers, counselors, and other school personnel; nor have the learning style and the learning rate of these students always been taken into account. The inclusion and encouragement of more students in science programs offer an important means of solving problems for individual students and of dealing with many of our societal requirements as well.

It also is evident today that the nation needs a scientifically literate population. All youth must have a background in science so that they can interpret their world adequately, make decisions about its future, and use this knowledge in many other aspects of their lives. It is hard to conceive of a future citizenry that can afford ignorance about genetic manipulation, computers, pollution, energy shortages, extreme population growth, poor nutrition, and other science-related problems. There are even simpler daily confrontations with life which present a need for some understanding of science. Among them are questions like these: What kind of fabric is this? What kind of fabric do I need for this purpose? What shall I do about insects in the greenhouse or garden? What about additives in food? What diet is best? What kind of fuel should we use? Why shouldn't I use a cyclamate? What are the effects, in terms of energy, of superhighways as compared to mass transportation?

What are the relative effects in terms of the environment? What do I need to develop my own film? What can I observe while backpacking?

On still another level, science is needed by the lay person less for its information than for its methodologies. In the study of science, attitudes and methods are developed which guide the student to gather related facts, organize them, select and try a procedure to solve the problem, and evaluate the results. This approach, unique to science, is useful in dealing with problems of all kinds.

Needs of this nature demand that careful attention be paid in school programs to every student so that he or she will acquire scientific knowledge and understanding of scientific procedures. We no longer can afford, nor is it now seen as inherently fair, to select a part of the school population for special attention. Science must be for everyone, and whatever means can be used to bring it to all students in a meaningful way should be explored. Literacy in science for all students means that each one should be helped to acquire learning skills, the freedom to pursue knowledge, and the ability to solve problems with confidence by knowing the processes to go through in the pursuit of solutions.

Science teachers face still another imperative in the 1970s: to interrelate the knowledge in subjects that have long been taught as separate units — biology, chemistry, physics — and to show students the linkages between science and subjects that are not part of the science curriculum — social studies, mathematics, engineering, the arts, and English. Knowledge in all these areas, although acquired in units, is intricately connected and integrated. Somehow, students must become aware of this in functional ways. Today's world and its problems demand responses which address total concepts and employ interdisciplinary attitudes and approaches. If integration of this kind cannot be implemented in the present classroom structure or administrative unit, some means of cooperation with other disciplines must be sought so that youth will understand complexities and unities of the world in which they live and begin to use this information in their work and in decision-making functions as citizens.

But why should science teachers devote time and effort in their science classes to career education? The answer lies in understanding career education's nature and purposes. Career education emphasizes the instrumental value of schooling for all students. It is a new focus in the classroom and not a new unit to be covered by each discipline. When it permeates regular classroom activities, it enhances the teacher's awareness of the lifetime needs of students, and it tends to heighten classroom interest in studies that once may have seemed dull and irrelevant to many students. The strong motivational power of career education stems from its application of learning to potential uses in the future work and other lifetime pursuits of students, and from its democratic recognition of each person's need to be recognized, considered, and readied for the responsibilities of adulthood.

In the science classroom, career education is an important tool. It can help teachers develop student interest in science careers and in the myriad careers related to science. It can motivate students to learn scientific procedures for use in other occupations and in their nonvocational pursuits. It can demonstrate the linkages among science studies and between science and other disciplines.

However, if science educators are to address themselves in an expanded way to the needs of a generation that faces a demanding future in terms of change and varied life-styles, they must begin to widen their own knowledge of possible careers for students and of the ways in which the requirements for those careers can be fulfilled. As a practical matter, they probably should devote a portion of their time to acquainting themselves with careers related to their subject content. Even the introduction of newspaper and magazine articles about a variety of careers — which should become part of the way of life in a science class — means that the teacher must develop an awareness of all potential career possibilities whether they are in a scientific or in a related field.

Application of the career education principle to science education requires the use of a wide variety of career examples to stimulate interest in science and scientific principles, and it necessitates use of career education as a part of the educational process rather than as an additive. For example, the teacher must pull together career information about the specific skills that students will learn in science classes and relate these skills to a broad array of career requirements. Within the science program, teachers are asked to identify, and then make known to their students, inherent skills and good work habits. Development of a sense of order, sequence, unity, and a recognition that things have beginnings, middles, and ends underlie the accomplishment of all work skills. Satisfaction in a job well done should get attention as an attitude worthy of emulation. Opportunities for self-motivation should be offered, recognized, and encouraged. The mastery of scientific skills should be put forward as a way of improving student opportunities in work or in the enjoyment of avocational interests. But these presentations must not be made in the form of abstract theorems or as bulletin board supplements. Career education must become a practicum in order to motivate most students.

Teachers should also be aware of the powerful influence their attitudes have upon students. There is little real value in giving lip service to a wide variety of appropriate work opportunities, then behaving as though the academic arena is the only place to spend one's life. The teacher's attitudes should reflect and emphasize that all kinds of work are praiseworthy and that, within each type of work, there are a number of avenues for continuing education and continued progress. In other words, teachers should demonstrate an open mind, be an informed resource, and offer positive encouragement and reinforcement in the career explorations of their students.

As for the uses of science in nonvocational aspects of life, teachers do not always clarify for students the pathways which science offers in the solution of problems or the relatedness of science to many everyday concerns. These relationships should be established by the teacher and not left to the chance that some students will discover a connection between solving classroom science problems and the methods they could expect to use in other situations, or the information they may need to make intelligent decisions as consumers or as citizens.

The question, then, about why science teachers should put any effort into career education resolves itself in these terms:

(1) Specific skills related to careers and to career selection will be identified.

(2) Identifying community resources as an element in career education can help to improve the educational process by bridging gaps between the school, the world of work, and the family.

(3) Teacher awareness of careers will increase as a result of thinking about a wide range of possibilities and involvement with a variety of student needs.

(4) Better relationships with students will result from a teacher's interest in contributing to the careers of all students, whether they plan to become scientists or to enter other occupations.

(5) The quality and amount of information about careers will be increased, giving students wider career options and better information about the choices they make.

(6) Student attitudes toward science will improve as a result of learning about the occupational and problem-solving aspects of science, which relate to many personal needs.

(7) For all students, the development of scientific reasoning processes and good work habits will carry over into a wide variety of careers.

(8) Science literacy can be achieved when students learn that knowledge of science is intimately related to their own well-being, and when they see for themselves in their career preparations some of the ways in which this is so.

Careers Directly Related to Science

To open up to more students the career opportunities in science and science-related occupations, and to help students decide whether they might like such careers, it is necessary to do some in-depth career exploration. The skills needed in various occupations — and at different levels in those occupations — should be identified. There are a great many other aspects of careers that also should be examined, among them: the satisfactions and disadvantages of an occupation, the life-style that an occupation will entail, the demand for workers in an occupation, the most common work sites for different jobs, the likelihood of constancy or change in an occupation during the student's working years, the promotional possibilities, and the student's own interests and capabilities in relation to career requirements.

In addition to speakers, library materials, brochures, field trips, and other typical means of providing career information, the science teacher should plan student activities which will integrate career education into their courses. The following are some exemplary activities that may be used for this purpose in giving students a good exposure to existing and future careers which are almost wholly dependent on a science education:

(1) Isolate a problem specific to your area of science. An example might be: Should Congress appropriate money to construct a sea-level canal across Central America?

(2) Spend some time with students in outlining different approaches to the solution of the problem.

(3) Identify the experts needed to solve the problem.

(4) Have students choose research tasks as part of working toward a solution. Cooperation with a government class on this project might call for the government class to conduct a mock congressional hearing in which testimony is heard from students in the science class.

(5) Finally, bring all students into a discussion of solutions that were arrived at and whether they think the decisions that were made are sound.

Another approach might be to have students study some aspect of the man-made world, such as the science or science-related careers involved in traffic safety. Students could gather data on the width of intersections, speed limits on approaching streets, the timing of each light, and then make decisions regarding "go" times, "stop" times, and whether a light is necessary. During this study, they could consult experts and learn how they make decisions and what kind of scientific preparation they had. If a particular intersection proves to be unsafe, students might also extend their activity into learning about the government and political implications involved in getting the situation corrected.

(1) Have chemistry students do a study of labels on containers in the kitchen, the cleaning closet, the medicine cabinet, the garden shed, and the home workshop. The assignment would be to learn something about a limited number of these substances. This task requires considerable detective work, for not all ingredients can be fully identified. However, those that are identified will fall into a number of chemical categories and will open many channels for discussion. Students will find out about the interrelatedness of chemistry with everyday life and with a wide variety of products. Their needs to learn more about chemical nomenclature will also be identified.

(2) Laboratory activities can be developed to show the specific role of career scientists. Some examples are:

(a) Fingerprinting, blood sampling, and drug analysis to find out about some of the common tasks of the crime laboratory scientist.

(b) A study of food adulterants, improper labeling, and poisons in various products to demonstrate the work of the Food and Drug Administration scientist.

(c) Soil sampling and study of drainage patterns to learn about the work of zoning engineers.

(d) Blood sampling, urinalysis, and other laboratory techniques to study the work of scientists in the health field.

(3) Occupations in the community might be studied by science students. What do a pharmacy, a grocery store, a photographic studio, the highway department, a hearing aid dealer, a television station, the parks department, a print shop, a hospital, a petroleum refinery have to do with chemistry? Or biology? Or physics? Students should make their own arrangements to visit some business or industry in the community individually or in small groups. Then they might present what they have learned to the class.

(4) Have students, with the help of family and friends, make a list of local practitioners in various science fields

who are willing to correspond with students on an individual basis to help students learn more about the nature of science careers. The information can be shared in the classroom and used by students to decide whether they have the inherent resources, interests, and attitudinal characteristics needed in the specific careers.

(5) Make arrangements for students to get some released time from school over a reasonable period of time to work with science practitioners, and to gather data and firsthand information on a particular career. (This should be a school-sanctioned program.) Schools can help students gain access to practitioners by developing an awareness of career education needs among parents and the local business community, and by maintaining lists of student sponsors and government programs through which some of these efforts might be funded.

(6) Give students a synopsis of the characteristics, constraints, and economic implications of various science careers. Have students decide what new careers might evolve from a particular career by the year 2000. Also, they might try to decide which existing careers will be defunct or of lesser importance by that year. This type of activity not only helps students determine their career options, but also to become aware of career linkages and opportunities for retraining.

(7) Provide students with a comprehensive problem that might be typical of a particular career. Ask them to try to solve the problem by communicating with people in different scientific areas — government, industry, and business — which relate to the problem. This activity will provide students with insight into the problems of communication within and across disciplines and will emphasize the interdisciplinary nature of many science careers.

(8) Have students make presentations — speeches and displays — at meetings of service clubs and other groups to relate what the students have learned about different careers and the contributions of workers in those fields.

This kind of activity gives students an opportunity to improve their communications skills and to enlist the community in their career exploration and skills acquisition efforts.

Careers Indirectly Related to Science

For those youth who are not heading into scientific careers, science needs are concentrated in three areas: in citizenship, in leisure activities, and in occupations in which science is only an element. Among the youth now studying science are some who take science courses simply to meet high school graduation or college entrance requirements. Too often this group passes through the study of science in a *pro forma* fashion. And when science teachers are overly concerned with developing specialists, they may perceive these students as peripheral to science.

Because career education is an integral part of teaching rather than a special course or a new unit, it enables the teacher to motivate and develop scientific literacy among all students without drawing time and resources away from the preparation of tomorrow's scientists. As humankind leaves the era of the industrial revolution and enters the postindustrial, technological age, the needs expand in nearly all aspects of life for scientific knowledge.

As citizens, all students will have to make many critical choices in complex issues revolving round scientific knowledge and affecting our planet. As consumers, they will be faced with making knowledgeable choices as to product content, content in relation to costs, and quality in relation to fuctional requirements. As workers, today's youth will need to be scientifically literate in order to function adequately as politicians, government workers, homemakers, plumbers, electricians, attorneys dealing with such matters as maternity suits or mineral rights, piano tuners, and acoustical engineers, and in many other occupational pursuits.

The homemaker, for example, should know about additives, preservatives, antidotes, chemicals marketed under a bewildering array of product names, and a host of other things used in the modern home.

Leisure time activities also call for scientific literacy. The gardener's hobby is a richer one, and carried out with greater efficiency, if the gardener understands the properties of various soils, the natural proclivities of plants, plant variations, insect functions in the plant world, fertilizers, and the like. A potting hobby is enhanced by knowledge of pigments as chemicals. The leisure time artist employs skills to better advantage with scientific use of acids, inks, dyes, metals, visual effects, and optical illusions. Many other leisure activities also are science related — camping, hunting, bird watching, rock collecting and polishing, metalworking, building a stereo system, and the like.

The alert teacher should know about these interests and try to relate them directly to science studies and activities. Not only does this emphasis help to focus the content of high school courses on career education, it also helps to capture student interest.

The following are some specific ways in which the science teacher can help students learn the relevance between their studies in the science classroom and their lives outside the school.

(1) The music instructor might bring a number of musical instruments to science class during a study of acoustics in physics. A comparison of stringed, woodwind, percussion, and brass instruments in terms of how sound is produced and modulated opens up many fields of discussion and investigation. It also shows students how science is related to leisure or occupational interests.

(2) Student research into the construction of football helmets — and the evolution that has taken place in their design — will have special interest for some students. They might explore the answers to these questions: Are modern helmets made of more protective materials than in the past? Are they protective enough? What are the characteristics of the materials used? In doing this research, students might ask the football coach to lend them a helmet now in use and samples of helmets used in the past. If the coach has a damaged helmet he is willing to discard, students might devise a series of tests on the helmet to get information on its resiliency, hard-

ness, brittleness, and other characteristics of the material. They might also ask the coach why he chose a particular helmet, and get specifications for the helmet from its manufacturer. In addition, they should relate their findings to broad areas of science — the use of plastics, testing, and the effects on the brain of sudden blows.

(3) The geodesic dome has become a popular structure for the construction of a shelter. Some of these domes are simply and inexpensively made. Students might build one and, in doing so, find answers to these questions:

(a) What is a geodesic dome?

(b) Where does one get information about these domes?

(c) Why are they considered a good form of shelter?

(d) What are their disadvantages?

(e) What is the dome's relation to such elements of science as geometric design, stresses, strengths of materials, cements, expansion and contraction, and the effect of sunlight on plastics?

The exercise may be of particular interest to students who are planning careers in construction, in real estate, assembly-line work, and a number of other fields which, although not in science itself, benefit from the application of scientific knowledge. The inquiry process also will help students learn how to handle difficult questions that they may not be able to answer unless they do some research.

(4) A major environmental problem, which has yet to be solved, revolves round oil spills in the oceans from tankers and from offshore drilling rigs. These spills do affect birds, sea life, and seashores. In investigating this problem, students might do these things:

(a) List the effects of oil spills.

(b) Select one specific life form and study the effects on that form. For example, if seagulls are selected, students should find out how oil harms a seagull, study the functions of feathers, learn if there is any way in which a gull can help itself if caught in an oil spill, and find out if there is any way that people can help seagulls caught in such circumstances. The students also might construct a model seagull with feathers from a poultry processor, fastening them on a cork base and then smearing oil on the feathers to learn firsthand what happens to bird feathers in this situation.

(c) Relate what has been learned to all applicable scientific principles.

(5) Motorcycles interest many of today's students. Although their maintenance can be delegated to experts who will keep a machine in good running order, a basic understanding of the working principles of a cycle allows even a novice to maintain the machine. Students in a motorcycle maintenance project might bring one of their cycles into the classroom where all students could help to:

(a) Identify the parts of the cycle and discuss their functions

(b) List these functions alongside pertinent scientific principles

(c) Investigate how each part can be adjusted to accomplish different results in the operation of a cycle

(d) Relate what has been learned to scientific knowledge (in terms of fuel, oxygen mixtures and combustion, metal parts vs plastic parts for certain purposes, purpose and function of lubricants, and the like)

The class might also invite someone from a local motorcycle repair shop to the classroom to explain the cycle parts, their functions, and how one knows what to do in repairing motorcycles (hypotheses) and the reasons (experience) for making these decisions (facts).

Strategies of these kinds can bring into the science classroom a multitude of experiences that will enable students to feel the pulse of science and examine its insides in ways that largely were possible for only a few students — those heading into science careers — before the advent of career education.

In chemistry courses where there is a good career orientation, students can learn not only that the food they eat, the water they drink, and the water they swim in are chemical compounds, but that they have roles to play as consumers, workers, and citizens. These are roles that call for knowledge of compounds and other forms of matter.

In a biology course, students will learn not only more about the functioning of their own bodies, how they have grown, and how to influence their own development, but also about biology as an occupational component and as a body of knowledge that is vital to their decision making as citizens. Moreover, they will learn more about the interdisciplinary relationships of knowledge and how they can employ this information in their daily lives.

These functions meet the imperatives of science today — that it became part of people's lives and not be an isolated body of knowledge, that it is able to encourage interest in its content among people who eventually will make many of the final decisions about its findings, and that it is able to demonstrate the vitality needed to draw into science and science-related pursuits a broad band of students who will bring with them rich resources of varied cultures and varied life experiences, and an earnest search for meaningful life roles.

Selected References

Chase, Craig C. "Employment Opportunities in the Environmental Field." *The Science Teacher* (February 1974), vol. 41.

Doughty, Ted G. "Career Awareness Education in Science." *Science and Children* (January 1975), vol. 12.

Dowell, Dorothy; and Dowell, Joseph. *Careers in Horticultural Sciences.* New York: Julian Messner, Publishers, Inc. 1969.

Ducat, Walter. *Guide to Professional Careers.* New York: Julian Messner, Publishers, Inc. 1970.

Dzurenda, Joseph V.; and Seltzer, Harold R. "Career Education in the Science Classroom: A New Approach to Teaching Science." *The Science Teacher* (May 1974), vol. 41.

Educators Progress Service, Inc. *Educators Guide to Free Guidance Materials.* Twelfth annual edition. 1973.

Evans, Rupert N.; *et al. Career Education in the Middle/-Junior High School.* Salt Lake City: Olympus Publishing Company. 1973.

Hawkins, Mary. "Office of Education Plans for a Marketable Skill for Every Student." *The Science Teacher* (December 1972), vol. 39.

Hoyt, Kenneth B.; *et al. Career Education and the Elementary School Teacher.* Salt Lake City: Olympus Publishing Company. 1973.

_____; *et al. Career Education: What It Is and How to Do It.* Second edition. Salt Lake City: Olympus Publishing Company. 1974.

Magliulo, Anthony. "A Career in Forensic Science." *The Science Teacher* (December 1972), vol. 39.

Miceli, Connie. "Minicourse on Careers." *The Science Teacher* (January 1974), vol. 41.

Millard, Reed. *Careers in Environmental Protection.* New York: Julian Messner, Publishers, Inc. 1974.

National Science Teachers Association. *A Career for You as a Science Teacher.* Washington, D.C.: National Science Teachers Association. 1966.

_____. "How Much Career Education in Science?" *The Science Teacher* (April 1973), vol. 40.

_____. *Keys to Careers in Science and Technology.* Washington, D.C.: National Science Teachers Association. 1973.

U.S. Department of Health, Education, and Welfare. *Minorities and Women in the Health Field.* Washington, D.C.: U.S. Government Printing Office. 1974.

3
Linking Mathematics Education to Career Education

National Council of Teachers of Mathematics

Thomas E. Long
Pennsylvania State University
University Park, Pennsylvania

Terry Shoemaker
Longmont, Colorado

Eugene P. Smith
Dearborn, Michigan

Marvin Veselka
Austin, Texas

James D. Gates
Reston, Virginia

3
Career Education
in the Mathematics Classroom

Mathematics is concerned with ideas, processes, and reasoning. It is a way of thinking, of organizing logical proof. It is an organized structure of knowledge with well-defined terms, symbols, and processes which develop its own beauty with its harmony, order, and consistency.

Commissions on the teaching of mathematics have identified the appropriate student goals as (1) knowing how mathematics contributes to understanding of natural phenomena, (2) knowing how to use mathematical methods to investigate, interpret, and make decisions in human affairs, (3) understanding how mathematics, as a science and as an art, contributes to our cultural heritage, (4) preparing for vocations in which the individual uses mathematics as a producer and consumer of products, services, and art, and (5) learning to communicate mathematical ideas correctly and clearly to others.

The classroom goal of a mathematics teacher is straightforward: to teach students mathematics. Mathematics teachers are constantly faced with decisions on how to teach the subject and how much emphasis to place on different topics. First, they must have a thorough knowledge of mathematics. Then they must determine which materials and activities are appropriate for the needs, interests, and abilities of their students. Many teaching techniques, applications, anecdotes, and even tricks and puzzles are used to help students learn mathematical concepts and skills. There must also be effective means for evaluating what has been learned. Interrelated among all of these decisions are the problems of managing the classroom and motivating students as they continue their adventure in mathematics.

Mathematics teachers have the opportunity not only to teach their disciplinary knowledge but to guide the learning of future scientists, engineers, craftworkers, people in the trades, and artists. Mathematics is involved in almost every problem in science, government, industry, trades, education, and the professions. New uses of mathematical ideas have furthered the development of science, the humanities, and the arts. Psychologists use mathematics to build learning models; social scientists use probability and game theory to study different aspects of society and the economy. Computers have extended the use of mathematics into space, politics, recreation, and educational instruction. Today all fields of knowledge are dependent upon mathematics. Probably no other subject has more universal application.

The good mathematics teacher therefore develops mathematical ideas and skills that students can use for further study, for everyday problems, and for personal satisfaction. Some students will be charmed by the logical consistency and beauty of mathematics. Others will enjoy the manipulation of numbers. However, for most, if the teacher fails to show how mathematics applies to other studies and interests, students are unlikely to transfer their knowledge of mathematics to other settings and will have less interest in the subject. Thus a major role of application is to motivate students. When students are shown how specific mathematical facts and skills can solve problems in the home and the community, in industry, in recreation, and in endless other ways, they are likely to try harder to learn. Career education is one way to motivate students and to provide linkages between the classroom and other life situations.

When concepts, skills, and real experiences are related to career education, they also provide opportunities for teachers to teach mathematics more effectively. The world of work is rich with mathematical problems that can become laboratory exercises for students to learn mathematics and problem solving. What better sources are there than those in the world around us?

For example, to help students understand vectors, the teacher could relate mathematics to vectors involved in an airplane flight and used by flight controllers. If students are to learn to interpret statistical graphs, they might use data and newspaper graphs which encompass current public issues. If students are to learn probability, they might look at how this applies to the work of insurance companies. Examples from the world of work can also help in the teaching of mathematical topics such as computation, measurement, statistical data, percentages, equations, geometric relations, ratio and proportion, estimation and approximation, and the use of computing machines. Another excellent way that career education can help in teaching mathematics is to have students identify mathematical problems related to the work of their parents, friends, or relatives.

Still another way in which career education can provide examples of mathematical applications is in the use of resource persons who work in the community — engineers, computer specialists, scientists — in business and in trades. Field trips to local businesses, industries, transportation centers, community institutions, or government agencies can enrich student knowledge of mathematical applications. Hands-on career education experiences with computers and calculators can also help teach mathematical concepts and skills. All of these career education applications in mathematical instruction are a means to an end. They serve to motivate new learning and to illuminate and clarify mathematics studies.

The main objective of mathematics teachers still is to teach mathematics. Career education can help the teacher do a better job of teaching by improving student motivation, satisfying student needs, providing application examples, and using community resources to reinforce classroom work. If the mathematics teacher is convinced career education can contribute to the principal objectives of the subject, then the fact that career education also helps to prepare students for success in the world of work is a highly attractive by-product.

Contributions of Career Mathematics

Mathematics is the entry gate to many occupations and professions. Knowledge of mathematics and facility in its application can enhance or limit the freedom a person has in making career choices. If a student wishes to become a scientist, a physician, an economist, an engineer, an airline pilot or navigator, for example, a thorough knowledge of academic high school mathematics is essential for entry into programs leading to these career goals. A knowledge of basic mathematics skills also is essential for success in many other careers that may not require post-high school education, such as restaurant waitresses, waiters, cashiers, or managers; insurance agents; retail clerks; sales representatives; machinists and pattern makers; carpenters or masons; nurses; and homemakers. In fact, discharging the responsibilities of an intelligent citizen is extremely difficult for anyone who lacks mathematical skills and concepts.

Occupational interests of the typical student begin to crystallize at approximately the ninth grade. At this point, the mathematical interests of learners and their perceptions of the mathematics competencies needed for occupational specialization begin to suggest some learning alternatives. Before the ninth grade, formal mathematics instruction was devoted chiefly to producing the basic computational skills for citizenship. But in the high school years, mathematics education begins to assume the mantle of occupational relevance for the individual learner.

For most people, a career exists only in retrospect. It represents the sum total of productive activities of the individual up to that point in time. To complicate matters further, the National Advisory Board for Vocational Education has found that, on the average, a worker in the United States can expect to change jobs about six times in his or her lifetime. In this climate, it is unlikely that any educational discipline can afford to be so specific as to prepare each individual perfectly for a particular niche in life. Rather, education must serve individual needs by helping to relate subject interests, learning experiences, and career alternatives to lifetime as well as immediate needs. This is particularly true of a subject area as pervasive as mathematics.

Career-relevant mathematics instruction should start before high school. Ideally, it will be offered from the child's first exposure in the primary grades to formal mathematics instruction. Beginning then, mathematics teachers should relate examples of the use of mathematics skills and their importance to work, in addition to teaching computational skills. But career-relevant mathematics should be emphasized at the high school level because this ends formal education for four out of five students. While the integrity of mathematics as a discipline is maintained, there must also be maximum consideration of the applications of mathematics in a wide variety of possible career choices.

Levels of Mathematics Competency in Careers

At least three levels of mathematics competency are identifiable in terms of the career relevance of mathematics as taught in the high school. These are not totally discrete levels but tend to blend and merge as they approach one another. The lowest acceptable level of mathematics competency should include mastery of at least the basic computation skills needed to function as intelligent consumers and citizens. These competencies should also include the skills needed in the creative use of recreation and leisure time.

The second level of mathematics competency has more than just a tint of individuality. It embraces both an understanding of mathematical concepts and capability in performing mathematical operations needed for satisfactory accomplishments of an occupation such as bank teller, physician, or physicist. In mathematics education at this level, teachers and learners both profit from understanding the learners' interests, capabilities, and ambitions. This knowledge, coupled with realistic occupational information which is available from a variety of sources, will enhance the opportunities for mathematics education to become relevant to individual careers.

The third level of mathematics competency relates to mathematically oriented professions — mathematician, actuary, statistician, mathematics teacher. These professions require extended study of mathematics and a high level of performance.

Even a cursory view of the situation indicates that making the teaching of mathematics relevant calls for attention to individual needs. Teachers, learners, mathematics programs, and society will benefit when these factors are recognized and internalized by those involved in the teaching and learning of mathematics.

Guidance Role of the Teacher

A study of the vocational choices of students who had high scores on the Indiana Mathematics Contest Examination turned up the fact that mathematics courses taken by these students were the most influential factor contributing to vocational choices of able students when they entered college. Parents were the second most influential factor in these choices. School guidance counselors exerted only a minor influence. These findings underscore the fact that mathematics teachers have a significant influence on the vocational choices made by students. Furthermore, if vocational guidance for students interested in mathematics is to take place, the high school mathematics teacher probably is the best prepared and most likely person to give it. This is an important but often neglected responsibility of the mathematics teacher.

It is easy to say that vocational guidance should be provided. But how can it be done? The remainder of this chapter will present some goals and strategies for accomplishing this objective. The focus is on career education to reinforce and motivate the learning of mathematical concepts, skills, and problem-solving strategies rather than on orienting teaching toward specific careers.

Teaching Models for Career Education

Career goals can be developed in many ways. This means that a teacher can be flexible in adapting a personal style of teaching to the implementation of career education. Not all topics will lend themselves to the same kind or degree of support of mathematics and career education goals. Some of the instruction may be most suitable for the development of career options. Then, the listing of possible career applications can help in teaching a given mathematical topic, concept, or skill.

At other times, there may be direct application of what is taught to specific careers.

Three possible models that teachers might wish to use to integrate career goals into the mathematics curriculum are given below. **Model A** relates mathematics at many levels to a variety of careers. In **Model B**, the exploration of occupations provides a stimulus to the student to seek an answer to the inevitable question: What mathematics skills and concepts are needed for these careers? **Model C** offers an example of how one feature of our society can be the stimulus for examining a number of career fields (the example used is the automobile).

Model A — *Relating subject or topical matter to a career*

These sample exercises include the use of geometry and algebra in the world of work.

Sample Exercise 1 — Geometry: Preparation for a career

This exercise is designed to help students see that geometry and its basic principles can be applied in their everyday lives and in preparation for their career aspirations.

A. Objectives and Concepts

1) General objectives

  a) To give the student experience in application of geometry skills in occupationally oriented learning activities

  b) To encourage the student to analyze personal abilities and interests as these relate to occupational areas studied

  c) To aid the student in working with the basic constructions in geometry

  d) To help the student tie basic constructions of geometry to design concepts

  e) To increase student awareness of possible work roles in the community relative to his or her characteristics

  f) To provide opportunities for the student to participate in the decision-making process

  g) To increase student awareness of reasons for taking geometry

2) Behavioral objectives

  a) The student will summarize, in written form, occupational information on at least one career area that uses geometry as a job skill.

b) Given a set of problems, the student will be able to make constructions with straight-line segments to an accuracy of 80 percent.

c) Given a set of problems, the student will be able to solve problems using angles to an accuracy of 80 percent.

d) The student will show reasoning and creative abilities by doing a project related to geometry. The project will be illustrated in either a physical or graphic construction.

e) At the end of this unit, the student will be able to name at least six career fields that use geometry as a job skill.

f) At the end of this unit, the student will be able to identify six geometric concepts or skills and apply these to the occupational area of his or her choice.

3) Concepts

a) Geometry is tied — directly and indirectly — into many careers, especially those of an industrial and engineering nature.

b) Geometric principles can be used in organizing information to solve everyday problems.

c) Geometry may be used to aid in logical thought processes.

d) Geometry is an indispensable tool of humankind.

e) Geometry originated in ancient Greece.

f) In 350 B.C., a Greek mathematician named Euclid compiled a set of rules concerning space and shapes that seemed so basic and true that no one seriously challenged it for nearly two thousand years.

g) The simplest concepts of geometry are points, line, and plane.

B. *Subject Matter*

Academic skills

1) English

2) Vocabulary terms in geometry:

point	chord
line	concentric circles
plane	adjacent
finite	perpendicular lines
infinite set	triangles
null set	equilateral

subset
intersection
union
assumption
collinear
bisector
radius

isosceles
scalene
right angle
obtuse angle
acute angle
reflex angle
undefined terms

C. *Occupational Information*

Fields using geometry skills:

Navigation
Automotive design
Architecture
Surveying
Engineering
Clothing design
Military service
Astronomy
Arts
Sheetmetal work
Map and chart making
Drafting
Construction
Sports
Lumber industry

Furniture design
Tailoring
Medicine
Oil drilling
Computer technology
Electronics
Landscaping
Communications
Scientific research
Interior design
Statistician
Law enforcement
Chemistry
Physics

D. *Study Activities*

1) Motivational activities

a) Have each student make a list of at least ten occupations in which geometry can be applied.

b) Conduct a class discussion on how geometry relates to different occupations.

2) Research activities

a) Have students bring clippings from magazines and newspapers showing how geometry is used in different occupations.

b) Have a resource person — engineer, builder, or sheetmetal worker, for example — visit the classroom to talk to the students.

c) Have each student prepare a written report on an occupation and tell how it relates to geometry.

d) Allow time for students to use occupational materials such as the *Occupational Outlook handbook*, SRA kit, Consumer Education Kit, and so forth.

3) Culminating activities

a) Have the students interview an individual in the occupation they researched and prepare a summary of the interview, telling at least one thing not known before the interview.

b) Encourage the students to become involved in the jobs they are interested in — perhaps helping a worker for a week — and prepare a report on this activity.

4) Evaluation techniques

a) Teacher self-evaluation

1. Did I plan effectively, using methods and materials wisely?

2. What degree of participation was generated by this unit?

3. Did I plan activities effectively to include each student to the best of her or his ability?

4. Did I cover all objectives set out at the beginning of the unit?

b) Observation of the student

1. Observed students' use of geometric skills as an individual and as part of the group

2. Observed for evidence of individual research and task completion

3. Observed for exhibited changes in student attitudes toward the subject area and the world of work

c) Written evaluation

1. The students will write reports on a vocation of their choice, using geometric skills.

2. The students will conduct a job interview and prepare a report after the job interview.

E. *Resource Materials*

1) U.S. Department of Labor, Bureau of Labor Statistics, *Occupational Outlook Handbook* (Bulletin No. 1650), Washington, D.C.: U.S. Government Printing Office.

2) Science Research Associates, Inc., SRA Occupational Exploration Kit, Chicago, Illinois.

Sample Exercise 2 — Algebra and careers

In business occupations, there is a broad use of mathematics. This example is one in which an office supervisor needs to find an algebraic solution to a problem:

It often is necessary in printing, manufacturing, and other kinds of production work to do cost analyses of various methods of turning out some particular product, publication, or item. For example, suppose that an office supervisor needs to provide copies of a noncopyrighted booklet for the staff. Copies of the booklet cost $1.00 each. A duplication service will make copies of the booklet for 15 cents ($0.15) per original page plus 1/2 cent ($0.005) for each sheet of paper. There are sixty pages in the booklet. At how many copies does it become more economical to use the duplication service? (Set up algebraically and graphically.) Clue: let x equal the number of copies desired and express the cost of the two different options (purchase or duplication) as y, a function of x.

Solution: x = number of copies desired

Cost (purchase) = $y = (1.00)(x) = x$ dollars

Cost (duplication) = $y = (0.15)(60) + (0.005)(60)(x) = 9 + 0.3x$

The equations to be graphed or solved simultaneously then are:

$$\begin{cases} y = x \\ y = 0.3x + 9 \end{cases}$$
$$x = 0.3x + 9$$
$$0.7x = 9$$
$$x = 12\text{-}6/7$$

Thus, after twelve copies, the student should duplicate:

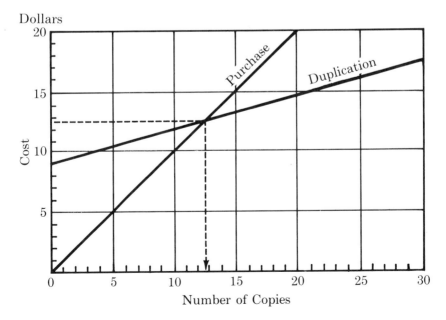

Model B — *Exploring the mathematics requirements of particular occupations*

These sample exercises prompt the student to look at the mathematical prerequisites that certain jobs require.

Sample Exercise 1 — Interior designer

A love of beauty has been a part of the human race since its earliest beginnings. One way this love is expressed is in home decoration. In the United States, the demand for interior designers has increased as we have achieved a more prosperous life-style.

Formal training is important, and it is required for membership in professional associations for designers. The designer must know historical periods and how to combine the contributions of each. Coursework consists of art, history, drawing, painting, architecture, sales ability, and business mathematics.

More than fifteen thousand men and women are engaged in full-time employment as interior designers. According to the "Career Guide" published by the National Society of Interior Designers, it is "almost impossible for soneone to enter the profession of interior design *without formal education* at an accredited college or university or professional school of interior design. Correspondence or home study courses are *not considered adequate formal education*" (emphasis added).

The mathematics one needs to become an interior designer depends upon the area of interior design a student wishes to enter and the school he or she plans to attend. The training may be at a two-year design school or in college work done that is aimed at a degree in engineering or fine arts. One should check the college or design school for entrance requirements.

To work as an interior designer, an individual must have the basic computation skills of addition, subtraction, multiplication, division, fractions, ratio and proportion, decimals, scale drawing, areas, and percentages. If students plan to enter an architecture or engineering school, the mathematics requirement will be greater, and they should plan to take two years of high school algebra, geometry, and any other advanced courses that are offered in mathematics.

Example one: The designer must be able to calculate the wall area in order to know how much material is needed for decorating.

Estimation for first problem: You are to estimate the cost of painting the four walls and ceiling of a room 30 by 26 feet, with a picture window 9 by 6 feet in one wall and two door spaces 3 feet by 6 feet 8 inches. The paint to be used costs $10.49 a gallon, and each gallon will cover 400 square feet. (Fractions of a gallon cannot be bought.) The ceiling is the standard height of 8 feet.

Estimation for second problem: The room is 29 by 17 feet, but the long walls are 12 feet high in the center, sloping to 9 feet at the ends. How much will it cost to paint the room? (All other facts are the same as for the first problem above.)

Example two: An industrial designer for an office furniture company compiles a specification sheet for a client. After talking to the client, the designer makes a rough sketch of the floor plan to scale, showing all wall placements or removals and the locations of all pieces of furniture necessary for the smooth operation of the business. Given a scale of 1/4 inch to 1 foot, find the following:

Item	Actual Measurement	Scale Measurement
Desk	48″ by 36″	_____
Desk	52″ by 42″	_____
Chair	24″ by 18″	_____
Chair	28″ by 22″	_____
Table	72″ by 36″	_____
File	14″ by 36″	_____
Bookshelves	20″ by 92″	_____
Couch	36″ by 76″	_____
End table	36″ by 18″	_____

Example three: Often it is necessary for an interior designer to decide how to cut fabric for an item to ensure minimum waste and the lowest cost in construction. This could include fabric for redoing furniture, for making draperies, or for any number of items to be placed in a home.

Problem: A customer wants a red, crushed velvet, hanging lampshade with gold swirl chord. The shade is 10 inches in diameter and 18 inches tall. The bolt of velvet fabric is 44 inches wide and costs $3.75 a yard. Should the shade be cut in one piece? Or would it be cheaper to cut it in two pieces and have two seams? Allow 1/4 inch on each piece for each seam and 1/2 inch at the top and at the bottom to form an overlap to secure the fabric to the frame of the lampshade.

Before cutting the fabric, the designer should draw a plan or make a pattern of less expensive material (bunting or broadcloth, for example) or of paper. In this problem, the designer should visualize the fabric as "unwrapped" from the cylindrical shade and would therefore need a rectangle of pattern material to begin the mathematical calculations of the exact dimension he or she will need when cutting the velvet fabric.

Sample Exercise 2 — Electronics technician

Today's electronics technician is as much a specialist as are doctors, lawyers, or engineers. All electronics technicians must reach a high degree of skill in fundamental concepts of the profession and the ability to manipulate the tools of the trade. They must be able to:

a) Identify component parts and determine their value

b) Read plans, blueprints, and schematic drawings

c) Read and use instruments such as ohmmeters, volt meters, ammeters, oscilliscopes, and frequency and time indicators

d) Analyze meter indications and compare them with calculated values to determine whether equipment is working properly

The electronics technician may be involved in production-line assembly and procedures, repair of existing equipment, prototype construction of new equipment, and installation of hundreds of different types of equipment, sales, and public relations.

Sample Exercise 3 — Other mathematics needs

During student interviews, it was noted that various mathematics skills were used. Different jobs had different mathematical requirements. These ranged from skills used by someone who repairs television sets to those used by lab technicians and circuit designers.

Many jobs required a strong mathematics background. Very simple problems involving addition, subtraction, multiplication, and division of integers and rational numbers often were used. Some areas of work involved percentages and units of measure. The metric system was often employed. Perhaps the chief mathematical tool used by a worker was basic algebra. Higher math skills were used by other workers, but these were in areas where additional training at a technical school or college would be required.

Example one: Computing voltage drops in a circuit

In a dc circuit, the sum of the voltage drops must be equal to the sum of the applied electromotive forces (emf). How much emf in the form of battery voltage must be added to a circuit which now contains emfs totaling 12 volts to meet requirements of the following voltage drops?

6.3 volts   3.2 volts   2.5 volts   3.7 volts

Example two: Computing total resistance in a series circuit

The total resistance of a series circuit is determined by the following formula:

$$R_t = R_1 + R_2 + R_3 + \cdots + R_n$$

Where n is the number of resistors.

In a college electronics experimental circuitry, the resistors of a circuit in series were found to be 1,500, 1,200, 1,472, and 570.63 ohms. What was the total resistance of this series circuit?

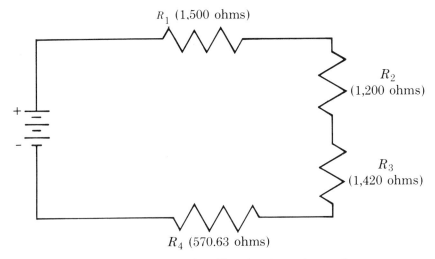

R_1 (1,500 ohms)

R_2 (1,200 ohms)

R_3 (1,420 ohms)

R_4 (570.63 ohms)

Example three: Computing illumination of a surface

The illumination on a surface that is not perpendicular to the rays of light from a source of light is given by the formula:

$$E = \frac{I \cos \phi}{d^2}$$

Where: E = illumination at point on surface (ft. candles)

I = luminous intensity of source cp (candlepower)

d = distance from source

ϕ = angle between incident ray and a line perpendicular to the surface

A certain 100 watt lamp has a luminous intensity of 108 cp. Compute the illumination at a point on a surface 10 feet from the lamp if the plane of surface is at an angle of 20 feet from the incidence rays.

$$\cos 20° = 0.9397$$

Model C — *Exploring the mathematics requirements in the automobile industry*

These sample exercises give the student an opportunity to learn the mathematics needed in a number of career fields that have developed as an outgrowth of a single phenomenon of our society — the automobile.

Sample Exercise 1 — The automobile industry

A consideration of the automobile industry — with its related occupations, problems, and benefits — will show that the industry has a great many activities in which mathematics is needed. The level of mathematics competencies that are used ranges from those acquired in high school to those acquired in college. Following is a list of occupations related to this industry:

Filling station attendant	Punch press operator
Gasoline truck driver	Tool and die designer
Car sales agent	Chemist
Auto mechanic	Quality control expert
Body shop worker	Statistician
Parts manager in repair shop	Electrical engineer
Truck driver	Metallurgical engineer
Bus driver	Chemical engineer
Race car driver	Mechanical engineer
Car painter	Industrial engineer
State highway patrol officer	Accountant
City traffic control officer	Actuary
Traffic engineer	Mathematician
Artist and designer	Computer specialist
Pattern maker	Automotive engineer
Assembly-line worker	

The following learning activities will help students in their investigation of careers related to the automobile industry.

a) Choose one of the occupations related to the automobile industry. Find out all you can about the occupation by reading, interviewing, and observing persons working in that occupation.

b) Ask yourself these questions:

1) Do I qualify for the job? If not, what will I have to do to prepare myself to qualify?

2) What is the pay?

3) What are the fringe benefits, such as insurance, retirement, and so forth?

4) What are the personal satisfactions?

c) Interview two or three people working in the occupation. Also interview the person who does the hiring.

d) Ask yourself these questions:

1) What chances are there for entry into a position with greater responsibility? For advancement in pay?

2) What service does the occupation offer to society?

3) Why is the job important?

e) Write a report on the information you learned about the occupation you chose.

Sample Exercise 2 — Automobile mechanic

The U.S. citizen, it has been said, has a love affair with the automobile. Working on cars to make them "come back to life" offers many personal satisfactions to anyone who likes to work with tools and machines.

In a survey by the Labor Department in 1974, skilled automobile mechanics employed by auto dealers in 34 cities had average earnings of $5.16 an hour. Mechanics are detectives who work with their hands. They have to diagnose problems then do the necessary repair work. A great variety of testing equipment is available to the mechanic. Among these are a motor analyzer, a spark plug tester, and a compression gauge.

Car mechanics usually work independently, without direct supervision. They must therefore have a sense of responsibility and the patience to stick to a job until it is done. Although most mechanics do repairs of all kinds, some become specialists. They may specialize in one type of work such as repairing transmissions, clutches, engines, generators, carburetors, electrical systems, air conditioning, or tuneups.

The following learning activities are designed to aid students in learning how mathematics is related to other aspects of the occupation of automobile mechanic.

a) From the accompanying price list, calculate the "bill" for a customer who has brought her car for a chassis lubrication and oil change (compute sales tax only on supplies and not on labor).

Labor	*Cost*
Chassis lubrication	$3.00
Lubricating wheel bearings (2)	5.50
Install oil filter	1.25
Oil change	(No charge)

Supplies	
Oil, brand x, per quart	$0.80
Oil, brand y, per quart	0.95
Oil, brand z, per quart	0.85
Gear lubricant, per pint	0.65
Oil filter	3.85

1) Chassis lubrication; oil change (five quarts of brand x); sales tax, 6 percent

2) Chassis lubrication; oil change (six quarts brand y); pint of gear lubricant; sales tax, 6 percent

3) Chassis lubrication; oil change (five quarts brand z); lubrication, front wheel bearings; two pints of gear lubricant in transmission; one pint of gear lubricant in rear end; sales tax, 6 percent

b) Many other mathematics exercises relating to the automobile can be developed — a study of road maps, the cost of owning a car, and the like. Information can be obtained from automobile companies and the U.S. Departments of Transportation and of Labor. The teacher will need to develop current, up-to-date data in these exercises. Teachers are encouraged to use their own ingenuity and imagination in efforts to visualize mathematics instruction by creating career relevant instructional materials.

Sample Exercise 3 — Mathematics applied to driving an automobile

The following data were collected on an automobile stopping distance at an auto test track:

s	10	20	30	40	50
d	5.3	22	50	86	139

Where:

s = the speed of the car in miles per hour (mph)

d = the sliding distance in feet

a) Plot the points on a rectangular coordinate system and then draw a smooth curve that seems to fit the data best. Clue: The curve of best fit may or may not pass through any of the plotted points.

b) Determine a formula, $d = f(s)$, for the curve drawn in (a) above. Clue: if $s = 0$, then $d =$ (what)? What kind of curve does the graph appear to be?

c) The normal driver's reaction time between a danger signal and the application of brakes is 3/4 second, the *reaction time* of the driver. The distance the car travels in this time is called the *reaction distance*. Write a formula $r = f(s)$ for the reaction distance if a car is traveling s mph.

d) Combine the answers from (a) and (b) above to write a formula for the *total* stopping distance, T, of a car traveling at s mph. T will include both the reaction and the sliding distances. Express T as a function of s.

e) Use the formulas to find d and T:

1) At 70 mph

2) At 35 mph

3) At 80 mph

4) At 100 mph

5) Do the answers in (1) through (4) above seem reasonable? If not, which do seem reasonable?

f) What is the approximate ratio of the sliding distances?

1) At 60 mph as compared to 30 mph

2) At 80 mph as compared to 20 mph

g) You are traveling at 70 mph and ready to overtake a car traveling at 50 mph. As you get within 100 feet of the car ahead of you, the driver suddenly slams on the brakes (because of an accident over a small rise in front of him).

1) Can you stop your car in time to avoid crashing into the rear end of the car preceding you if the driver stops it as quickly as possible? (Assume the information in this set of exercises to be correct and that because of traffic conditions, you cannot get out of your lane of traffic.)

2) If you can stop in time, how far will you be from the car ahead when you stop?

3) If you cannot stop in time, approximately how fast will you be traveling when you hit the rear of the car ahead?

h) Write a formula for the approximate relationship between f (feet per second of a car) and s (speed in mph). The formula should be simple enough that a driver can easily use it as he drives along the highway.

Summary

The role of the high school mathematics teacher is truly significant when the nation's students are attempting to make career choices. Many girls have felt that careers in which mathematics is basic or essential were open chiefly to boys. Today, more than ever before, there are widening opportunities in these careers for both girls and boys, and to those from minority groups. And as teachers work to develop high school mathematics courses that are relevant to careers for today's youth, they will widen the interest of youth in mathematics courses. In addition to being a mode of thought and reasoning, mathematics will take on a newer dimension — a system of thought and reasoning that has important, direct relationships to the lives and careers of most students.

Selected References

American Mathematical Society. *Professional Training in Mathematics.* Providence, Rhode Island: American Mathematical Society. 1972.

_____. *Seeking Employment in the Mathematical Sciences.* Providence, Rhode Island: American Mathematical Society. 1973.

American Statistical Association. *Careers in Statistics.* Washington, D.C.: American Statistical Association. 1974.

Chronicle Guidance Publication, Inc. *Mathematical Technician.* Moravia, New York: Chronical Guidance Publications, Inc. 1974.

_____. *Mathematician.* Moravia, New York: Chronical Guidance Publications, Inc. 1972.

_____. *Why Not Mathematics?* Moravia, New York: Chronical Guidance Publications, Inc. 1971.

Employment Development Department, Mail Control Unit. *Mathematician.* Sacramento, California. 1969.

Mathematical Association of America. *Professional Opportunities in Mathematics.* Washington, D.C.: Mathematical Association of America. 1974.

Mathematician. Largo, Florida: Careers. 1972.

National Council of Teachers of Mathematics. *Mathematics and My Career.* Reston, Virginia: National Council of Teachers of Mathematics. 1971.

Scientific Manpower Commission. *Science and Engineering Careers: A Bibliography.* Washington, D.C.: Scientific Manpower Commission. 1974.

_____. *Test Yourself for Science.* Washington, D.C.: Scientific Manpower Commission. 1971.

Society for Industrial and Applied Mathematics. *Careers in Mathematics*. Philadelphia: Society for Industrial and Applied Mathematics.

Society of Actuaries. *So You're Good at Math*. Chicago: Society of Actuaries.

University of Toronto, Guidance Centre. *Mathematics*. In *The Student, Subject, and Careers*. Toronto, Ontario: University of Toronto. 1974.

U.S. Department of Labor, Bureau of Labor Statistics. *Employment Outlook for Mathematics Occupations — Mathematicians, Statisticians*. Washington, D.C.: U.S. Government Printing Office. 1974–75.

_____. *Employment Outlook for Teaching Occupations*. Washington, D.C.: U.S. Government Printing Office. 1974–75.

_____. *Math and Your Career*. Washington, D.C.: U.S. Department of Labor. 1974.

4
The English Language: Basic to Any Career

National Council of Teachers of English

Dorothy Davidson
Texas Education Agency
Austin, Texas

Mildred Dougherty
Louisville Public Schools
Louisville, Kentucky

Jesse Perry
San Diego City Schools
San Diego, California

Seymour Yesner
Minneapolis Public Schools
Minneapolis, Minnesota

Marjorie Farmer
School District of Philadelphia
Philadelphia, Pennsylvania

4
Career Education in the English Classroom

English teachers and others in the profession are constantly in the process of defining the discipline that we Americans call "English." Indeed, the subject with the highest program priority at the next convention at the National Council of Teachers of English is "What Is English?" During the last decade, definitions have included (1) academic proficiencies — language, literature, and composition; (2) fundamental skills — listening, speaking, reading, and writing; and (3) basic communication competencies — literacy and verbal skills.

By questioning its own purposes, the English profession recognizes that work must continuously be reassessed, redirected, and reviewed as its living context changes. And as the profession develops and employs this capacity for self-assessment, with its implied dimension of freedom and courage to make changes as a result of new insights, the process of definition becomes a significant element in any truly comprehensive description of what "English" is.

But changes in definitions have not altered the profession's core concerns. A primary concern is to give learners at the high school level an opportunity to achieve language communication competencies that will equip them for the responsibilities of adulthood. A major responsibility of the adult is to do work that yields both personal fulfillment and service to the common good. Further, the English program seeks to prepare learners to participate creatively in the life of the world community. These are career purposes, and they are the purposes of the teaching of English.

Yet as English teachers consider the career-oriented teaching of English, they have been trying to resolve for themselves at least three major professional questions:

(1) What is the relationship between the humane and the practical uses of English?

(2) Where is the balance between the obligation to teach standard English and the importance of valuing linguistic differences?

(3) What are implications in the teaching of English of varying career goals?

The task of reconciling the humane uses of English with the practical applications of English is basic in the profession. The humane uses are to help students define and enhance the self and achieve healthy interaction with others. The practical uses are the means by which the self is presented and by which dynamic interaction with others is achieved. These are specific skills needed for functional, practical literacy — job applications, employment résumés, interviews, public speaking, and other forms of informational and persuasive communication. A career education emphasis in English can help clarify the interdependence that unites these humane and practical functions.

A related professional concern of English teachers is maintaining the necessary balance between the obligations to teach the conventions of standard, written, Americanized English and the importance of valuing varying linguistic styles of learners. English teachers increasingly are recognizing the interdependence of these two aspects of language — that it is only on the underlying structure of each learner's unique "languaging" power, with its special style and content, that the learner can build a widening range of sophisticated linguistic strategies.

But the teaching task is not a simple one. If too much stress is placed on one side, the richness of various cultures and the interest of many persons in English studies may be closed off. If too much stress is placed on the other side, students may fail to learn skills that will enable them to communicate well with other people and that they may need to get certain types of work and to progress in their careers. Obviously, the profession must find ways to open access to standard Americanized English for learners from all language communities without denying the value and strength of linguistic styles emerging from their own cultural heritage.

A third concern of the profession is how to open career options to students in a new perspective, one in which the preparation for higher education and the preparation for technical and other occupations stand on equal footing. Past imbalances and the valuing of classroom work for the college bound over that provided for the general or terminal student were the result of the differential status historically assigned these groups in society and of the fact that schools are run by people who themselves are products of higher education. But increasingly, financial rewards are being equalized among different types of employment, and greater regard is accorded the societal contribution of each. Some of the factors that have helped bring these changes about are the numbers of middle-class high school and college dropouts, welfare recipients' and prisoners' rights movements, fair employment practices, legislation accompanied by affirmative action requirements, efforts to provide compensatory education, more sophisticated labor-management negotiations, and the extended participation of people in the process of government.

As the English teaching profession addresses these questions of content and student needs, it does so in full awareness that high schools as they now exist often seem to fail in their services to the young. English, as a humane and liberating discipline, can make major contributions to the education profession in achieving a clearer sense of the equal dignity of all students and in helping young people find ways to achieve personal growth and motivation in the English classroom. Career education is one of the important means by which these contributions can be made.

What Is Career Education?

Career education has brought about a new perspective on what a career is. In the context of education, a career no longer connotes a job that has a particular societal stature, or one in which people have special training, or one that is likely to be a person's livelihood for an entire lifetime. It does not even mean work for which a person gets paid. Instead, the concept of career now embodies — at least in the minds of career educators — far-reaching consequences of life-style, commitment, involvement, and self-fulfillment. While some people still regard careers as limited to that part of life connected with work, career educators see a career in terms of a continuing search for a satisfying and fulfilling life.

For the high school English teacher, these redefinitions in no way conflict with the intuitively perceived values underlying the work in English classes. In fact, if career education is the process by which individuals shape and control their destiny with some concurrent measures of personal satisfaction and societal contribution, English should become a valuable resource to everyone because of the power it bestows on individuals to see into themselves and others and to manage their affairs with competence and affability. English also contributes in a more specific way to career education through its emphasis on communications skills. Most productive activities involve communication among human beings. Most instructions in paid employment must flow through spoken and written language. All human relations is communication. And all jobs that are not primarily manual are almost entirely communicative — the transmission of ideas, orders, and messages.

To determine whether these career education needs of students actually are being met in the English classroom, one must appraise present teaching methods and content. Then the teacher can decide what should be perpetuated, what should be altered, and what should be eliminated. Some questions that should be raised in the course of this appraisal are:

(1) Is the instruction elitist, and does it tend to favor a small group of students, or does it serve a broad student population well?

(2) Does the teacher, by acknowledging and developing natural linguistic proclivities, help students develop their vocabularies, learn the subtleties of words, perceive relationships, stretch their minds, and engage in a variety of ways of thinking so that they can fully explore their potential, their options, and the world in which they live?

(3) Is the instruction pertinent to experiences and events in everyday life so that it is relevant to student concerns and gives students a way to interpret and express their own experiences?

(4) Does the classroom develop skills which will enable students to argue ideas with themselves and with others in order to clarify their thinking and values and to resolve problems?

(5) Are students achieving functional literacy — the ability to read and write according to their functional needs in school and in the world of work?

(6) Is the English classroom helping students know themselves and know others — not just as casual beings who pass this way but once, but as human beings with whom there are shared experiences and understanding?

(7) To cultivate such knowledge, is full use being made not only of literature but also of role playing, theater, and expressive areas such as journalism, speech, debate, film, and dance?

(8) Is English more than a simple tool for other subjects — is it a base on which students can build realistic approximations of their social, vocational, and environmental roles, and will it help them make choices leading to satisfying and fulfilled lives?

When these questions can be answered in the affirmative, English becomes not a device for screening out students according to some prefabricated notion of winners and losers in collegiate or in classical career terms, but a means for instructing all students in a purposeful, pleasurable classroom which uses the past and anticipates the future. However, to say all of this does not assure that English will be well taught or that methodology and content will always mesh in such a way that they will be perfectly and immediately clear to all students. But it is a probability, if not a certainty, that energizing students round their perceived interests and needs (even when these are self-centered or ultimately erroneous) will motivate students, help them find matters of consequence to themselves in the English classroom, and develop in larger numbers of students greater linguistic competence.

Career Education Goals

In incorporating career education in English studies, certain goals should be established which are aimed at helping students achieve economic independence, appreciate the dignity of work, learn about the satisfactions of work, and acquire the ability to make wise decisions about career options and choices. The following goals are stated in terms of students who complete the high school English program. These students should:

(1) Have the linguistic knowledge and skills necessary to become employable, to continue education throughout a lifetime, and to pursue developing vocational and avocational career interests

(2) Have increased self-awareness and direction, expanded career awareness and aspirations, and appropriate attitudes about the personal and social significance of work and careers as a result of clarifying their values through literature and other English disciplines

(3) Have decision-making skills necessary for future long-range career planning, particularly in English-related careers and in other careers where linguistic ability is an important skill

The following sample objectives and learning activities may suggest to the English teacher how the content of the English program can carry out these goals for career education.

Objectives for Goal One

In the following exercises, students will (1) discover what it is like to work in various occupations related to English; (2) develop flexible reading rates, according to the difficulty of the material and the purposes for reading, and will generalize this skill to specific materials; (3) recognize that different kinds of written communication, ranging from simple messages to technical reports, are important components in various careers; (4) use language, spoken and written, in different ways, depending upon the purposes, situation, and audience; (5) experience vicariously a variety of roles through literature which exemplifies different attitudes, values, and dilemmas of the human condition; and (6) make careful observations and interpretations of the content and language requirements of various communications media, including films, audiotapes, television, magazines, newsletters, newspapers, sales letters, posters and billboards, and public speeches.

Sample Exercise 1 — Various occupations related to English

a) Students will list the names of several people in literature or in real life who have been successful in different occupations related to English. By reading biographies, newspapers, or other research sources, students will get information so that they can describe some of the factors that led to the success of these persons.

b) Students will write essays on occupations related to English, describing such characteristics as opportunities in those fields, number of persons now employed in these occupations, requisite skills and personal characteristics, educational and training requirements, pay, possibilities for promotion, advantages and disadvantages, work sites, degree of supervision and of independence, and places in the community where such workers are employed.

c) Students will write essays illustrating the application of language study to careers of their choice. These essays should also include the reasons why they are interested in these careers, their personal likes and dislikes which will affect their work in that career, their pertinent skills, and in-depth information on the characteristics and opportunities in the career field.

Sample Exercise 2 — Developing flexible reading rates

a) Students will play roles in job interviews and in other career-oriented situations.

b) Students will observe — by audiotape, film, or television, in offices or through simulation — various communication techniques used by adults in their work.

c) Students will discuss effective and ineffective uses of verbal and nonverbal communication.

d) Students will collect experiences, through interviews and other means, which show the variety in interpersonal communication among workers in specific occupations.

Sample Exercise 3 — Recognizing many different kinds of written communication

a) Students will study specific occupations to determine the amount and the kind of reading and writing skills which are needed; if possible, they should collect samples of writing by workers in these occupations.

b) Students will demonstrate an understanding of a variety of written communications in the world of work by producing an array of these communications and identifying where they are used and why they are needed.

c) Students will assemble and examine a variety of written communications from a single work site, such as a business office.

d) Students will evaluate the written communications of their peers as a means of strengthening their understanding of what they and their fellow students know and what they still must learn.

Sample Exercise 4 — Using language, spoken and written, in different ways

a) Students will play roles and compare language in the following situations: class discussions, peer group discussions after school, student-adult discussions in a civic situation, and peer group interaction in a variety of social situations.

b) Students will produce samples of written language which is appropriate in several situations — from one class to another about a joint project, among peers about a social occasion, from adult to student to adult about a school issue.

Sample Exercise 5 — Experiencing a variety of roles

a) Students will read fiction, essays, biographies, and autobiographies to determine how values and attitudes can shape decisions.

b) Students will analyze characters in their readings to illustrate the components of individual personality, and the role that these play in human interaction.

Sample Exercise 6 — English in the communications media

   a) Students will analyze the communications media for use of persuasion devices.

   b) Students will analyze political speeches that represent different viewpoints. They will report the facts presented, the weight given to various facts, and interpretation of facts.

   c) Students will participate in the filming or taping of commercials or short narrative accounts of a football game, an accident, an environmental hazard, a school election campaign, and the like, and will adapt their presentation to the subject content, media form, and audience.

Objectives for Goal Two

In the five sample exercises below, students will (1) develop a systematic method to clarify their values; (2) demonstrate how their values, abilities, interests, aptitudes, and attitudes are compatible with a variety of occupations and careers; (3) become aware of the personal significance that work and careers have for the individual; (4) learn ways that theater, film, radio, and other communications media offer a variety of experiences for personal growth, occupational satisfaction, and recreation; and (5) try to determine which values tend to be generative and to produce other values.

Sample Exercise 1 — Systematic method of clarifying values

   a) Students will study a value hierarchy and illustrate it, using values discovered in a novel or short story. (Use the following format to show how values are built.)

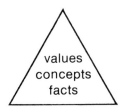

   b) Students will apply a value hierarchy to the situations that follow:

   1) A student-developed dialogue   4) A television program

   2) A filmed or taped commercial   5) A magazine article

   3) A magazine advertisement

Sample Exercise 2 — Values, abilities, interests, aptitudes, and attitudes

 a) Students will write essays illustrating the application of values, abilities, interests, aptitudes, and attitudes to specific career choices.

 b) Each student will take an interest inventory, structure a profile, and analyze the profile for its accuracy in guiding him or her toward a career choice.

 c) In a group effort, students will analyze the structure and content of an interest inventory.

Sample Exercise 3 — Personal significance of work and careers

 a) Students will analyze anecdotal accounts, such as newspaper interviews with interesting persons, to learn the personal significance of work and careers for various people.

 b) Students will explore, through interviews, differing values held by individuals regarding their work, and will invite guest speakers to the classroom, see audiotapes made at work sites, and the like.

 c) Students will write essays or participate in a panel discussion on the role that a career plays in the development and nurturing of self-concepts.

Sample Exercise 4 — Nonprint media and personal growth, occupational satisfaction, and recreation

 a) Students will role play, construct dialogues, and film and tape their dialogues, illustrating the value of nonprint media in personal growth and social diversion.

 b) Students will explore facilities in the community, including an educational television channel, different kinds of movie houses and radio stations, and community theater groups.

Sample Exercise 5 — Values that produce other values

Assess the following statements in terms of whether they generate other values.

 a) Seeking for goals and for answers to problems is a person's destiny and should be construed as valuable and pleasurable in and of itself.

 b) Knowing about the world as realistically as possible is good.

 c) Having the power to express oneself according to one's urges and needs is self-enhancing.

d) Having the ability to project one's understanding into the lives of other creatures is powerfully liberating and self-sustaining.

e) Being able to absorb oneself imaginatively and sympathetically with others and with their problems is revitalizing and often necessary.

f) Wanting and being able to communicate with others is sustaining of one's own sense of worth and of one's assurance of place in a community.

g) Having a sense of security as a result of work, social place, and communication with other people relieves one of fear and alienation.

Objectives for Goal Three

The objectives for this goal are threefold: (1) to make and analyze career decisions on the basis of a decision-making model which includes consideration of rewards, costs, alternatives, and personal values; (2) to be able to gather information regarding career choice through reading, interviewing, observing, and other communicative means; and (3) to be able to use knowledge of oneself and of careers as one makes tentative career choices.

Sample Exercise 1 — Making and analyzing career decisions

a) Students will choose occupations in which there are generalists and specialists, interview these workers in terms of job satisfactions and dissatisfactions, and write an analysis of their findings.

b) Students will search for answers to such questions as:

1) What do newspaper reporters and printers do?

2) How do they write, edit, and print the news?

3) What do other staff members do?

c) Students will visit a local newspaper establishment to talk to workers, examine the newspaper, and produce a class paper on careers in journalism.

Sample Exercise 2 — Gathering information on career choices

a) Students will interview adult workers and describe how life experiences have affected their career development.

b) Students will locate sources of information regarding selected careers, including the school library and school counseling office, and sources in the community — private and public employment agencies, computerized information services, vocational education centers, and community colleges.

Sample Exercise 3 — Using knowledge of themselves and of careers to make tentative career choices

a) Students will prepare a résumé and portfolio about themselves, including creative or informative writing they have done and other types of communications (photo essays, cartoons, graphics) which may be useful in helping their parents, counselors, vocational educators, prospective employers, college entrance interviewers, and themselves to determine appropriate career channels and choices.

b) Students will use language in classroom situations often enough to gain experience in talking effectively about their career interests and their personal strengths.

Implementation Strategies

How should the English teacher go about developing a career-oriented curriculum of this kind? Of course, the teacher may work apart from colleagues, incorporating ideas gained from this chapter and other materials into course plans. But the going may be easier if the teacher works with colleagues within the English department and across departmental lines, particularly if the school has outside consultation services, a library of resource materials, and other supports for a curriculum development program. But whether the teacher works alone or with others, the following steps are appropriate in implementing career education goals in the English classroom:

First, formulate goals, objectives, expected outcomes, and evaluation plans. A number of resources may be drawn upon — guides from other schools, bulletins developed in state departments of education and career education projects, articles in the *English Journal* and other professional magazines, and the like.

Second, identify instructional resources. The English teacher may know the community served by the school and be able to identify individuals, groups, businesses, industries, professional and service organizations, and institutions that can provide information useful to English students. There may be available a master list of community resources from which to draw much of this information. Students themselves are an important resource, and their involvement in planning, sharing, and developing ideas on career education in the English class-room should be used creatively.

Teachers in the school from vocational education, social studies, fine arts, foreign languages, and other disciplines should be added to the resource pool. Parents and other family members are also sources of information on a wide variety of occupations and on career values, aspirations, and decision-making processes. All of these efforts may result not only in a good career education program but also in opening up good lines of communications between the English classroom and other departments in the school, and between the school and the community.

Third, make decisions on program elements. Having established goals, objectives, expected outcomes, and evaluation plans for a career-oriented program, the English teacher is ready to decide on the changes needed in existing courses, their organization, and their content. New courses may be needed, although the infusion of career education concepts in all courses, new or old, is more readily defensible than adding a new course in the school curriculum — and it probably accomplishes more.

If the implementation effort includes the entire department, the English teacher should assist in making decisions about staffing a career-oriented program. Alternative staffing patterns may build upon strengths and competencies of individual teachers. Team teaching and cooperative arrangements crossing departmental lines both for planning and teaching may make the best use of competencies. Resource persons from the community may further enrich the instructional plans. The objective should be to seek out and find ways to use the best possible persons to get a career education emphasis to supplement the competencies of each English teacher, and to broaden the perspective of students with real-life experiences relating to careers, work-oriented values, and career decision making.

The English teacher engaged in the process of developing a career-oriented program should also explore how a simple broadening of perspective can help bring about a good career education focus. For example, in connection with the various strategies that the teacher already uses to explore a student's interests, background of experience, values, attitudes, and competence in the language arts, the teacher might also begin to gather information, observations, and impressions that are important to career development. What work experience have individual students had? What are their views of work? What are their career aspirations at the moment? Answers to these and other questions begin to round out for the English teacher a better view of each student, which can serve as a basis for individualizing plans for a career-oriented program.

In summary, even as the teaching of English undergoes redefinition, its inherent purpose is steadfast: to give students the opportunity to achieve communications competencies to serve them as adults in seeking personal fulfillment and service to the common good, and in participating creatively and effectively in the life of the community.

Career education, broadly defined, can penetrate the content and the methodology of the high school English program at a time when students are seeking clarification of their personal values and are facing the need to make career decisions. The English classroom can become a laboratory in which to explore communication in its many forms and to prepare for effective and satisfying communication with other people. These are vital skills, whether they are used in work, in leisure, or in both.

Selected References

Gordon, W. J. J. *The Metaphorical Way of Learning and Knowing.* Cambridge, Massachusetts: Porpoise Books. 1971.

Hawley, Robert C.; *et al. Composition for Personal Growth: Values Clarification through Writing.* New York: Hart Publishing Company, Inc. 1973.

Parnes, S. J. *Creative Behavior Guidebook.* New York: Charles Scribner's Sons. 1967.

Prince, G. M. *The Practice of Creativity: A Manual for Dynamic Group Problem Solving.* Evanston, Illinois: Harper & Row. 1970.

Raths, L.; *et al. Values and Teaching: Working with Values in the Classroom.* Columbus, Ohio: Charles E. Merrill Books, Inc. 1966.

Shaftel, Fannie. *Role-Playing for Social Values.* Englewood Cliffs, New Jersey: Prentice-Hall, Inc. 1972.

Washington State Coordination Council for Occupational Education. "Who Am I? Where Am I Going? How Do I Get There? A Guide for Career Awareness." Seattle: Washington State Coordination Council for Occupational Education.

(Film)

"Judging from Language." 16mm, 20 minutes. Washington, D.C.: Bono Film Services. The film raises questions about effect of a nonprestige dialect in a job interview, but it offers no answers.

5
Social Studies and Its Career Implications

National Council for the Social Studies

Brian J. Larkin
National Council for the Social Studies
Washington, D.C.

Mary T. Strong
Lexington, Kentucky

Harold E. Oyer
Sewickley, Pennsylvania

Florence Jackson
New York, New York

Dean Moore
Cincinnati, Ohio

5
Career Education
in the Social Studies Classroom

Social studies is the interdisciplinary study of people and their society. As such, social studies focuses on the individual as a social being, on an analysis of society, and on the relationship between the two. Drawing its material and methodology from the social sciences, the humanities, and more recently the physical sciences, social studies has three broad objectives:

(1) To acquaint students with the societal process, most often under the general label of "citizenship education"

(2) To teach the cognitive content, concept, skills, work approaches, attitudes, and values of the social studies disciplines

(3) To help students grow and develop as individuals by acquiring information, tools, and value systems through their studies

The content of social studies is becoming increasingly significant at the high school level. In large part this is a result of the rapid social and economic changes taking place in society. To deal with these changes, the individual — whether as worker, consumer, or voter — must understand what is happening and why. But what does social studies have to do with career education?

This question is often asked. It seems to stem from a misconception that career education is simply another name for vocational training. However, when career education is recognized as a concept dedicated to helping everyone learn "the values of a work-oriented society, to integrate these values into their personal value systems, and to implement these values into their lives in such a way that work becomes possible, meaningful, and satisfying to each individual" (Hoyt *et al.*, 1974, pp. 15, 100), some of the linkages between social studies and career education begin to appear.

In a broad and profound sense, social studies and career education are intimately related. Both seek to prepare the young for a way of life that is not only constructive but offers personal fulfillment. A position statement in 1972 by the National Council for the Social Studies said, "Social studies education has a twofold purpose: The enhancement of human dignity through learning, and a commitment to rational processes as the principal means of attaining that end." Kenneth B. Hoyt, who has written extensively on the subject of career education, has described it in these terms: "Career education is the totality of experiences through which one learns about and prepares to engage in work as part of her or his way of living."

Both social studies and career education are concerned with helping the young to become adults who can cope and who are able to deal successfully with changing societal patterns and requirements, able to exert freedom of choice, and able to accept responsibility. Both recognize the importance of personal development — the need to arrive at an understanding of self and a sense of personal worth which are grounded in the knowledge that each individual is important to society and can command the respect of his or her fellow humans.

The principles and knowledge concerning human growth and human relationships that the social sciences have built as a result of extensive research in recent decades will enable teachers to guide students through a gradual developmental process. The teacher is important in helping students achieve insights about their abilities, limitations, attitudes, aspirations, interests, and potential, and in helping students see the congruency of these personal characteristics with needs in various occupations. Basic to all career education, the strengthening of skills for making such assessments can be a major contribution of social science teachers in the career preparation of their students.

To be sure, social studies and career education each has its own areas of specialty. Career education, for example, is primarily concerned with one portion of an individual's life — the work segment — and much of its content (the development of work attitudes, specific abilities, and skill levels) is only tangentially related to social studies. However, as social studies and career education move toward their own objectives, they tend to enhance one another.

Social studies offers youth a broad background against which to measure personal decisions on occupational options and the life-styles that these may entail, while career education can introduce the relevancy of personal interest into the social studies classroom. If teachers can show students that social studies has something to do with the world the students perceive — if we can relate what we are teaching to the kinds of problems they have, to the experiences they seek, to the needs they feel, and to some of their career options — what we teach has greater meaning. As Roy Price observed in the 1969 yearbook of the National Council for the Social Studies: "Learning may be a matter of discovering a personal meaning, and teaching may be a process of helping the individual develop personal meaning."

Although career education is not the only way to help students find personal meaning in social studies, it can indeed be a major one, and can reinforce student interest in social studies content. The remainder of this chapter gives social studies teachers more detailed information on career education, and it offers ideas and tools that will be useful in relating their teaching to developing occupational knowledge and goals among their students.

Contributions of Social Studies to Career Education

Does social studies have a payoff in dollars and cents? What can one do with social studies aside from teaching? Are there any career implications for most students who take history, economics, or other components of the social studies?

The real return to the student career interests is less specific than what students can learn in auto mechanics or computer programming classes — nevertheless, the return may be great. Many of the attitudes, values, and cognitive knowledge and skills that can be acquired in the social studies classroom are extremely important in the occupational life of most workers, as well as in their social, political, and family lives. This is because learning about work goes far beyond skills preparation for a particular job. It involves intellectual strategies that are a key part of the social studies approach — inquiry, value clarification, problem solving, and decision making. It involves questions about how individuals relate to their job, what they bring to it, what it does for them, what they see in it, and what they take from it.

Some of the questions students must explore during their consideration of adult careers are these:

(1) What is my quality of performance or level of productivity, and how does this affect my potential for various occupations?

(2) Am I satisfied with the tasks called for in an occupation — are they above or below my ability and my expectations?

(3) Can I handle the routine, monotonous, and demanding tasks which are an element in most jobs, no matter how attractive the jobs seem to be?

(4) Do I know what it takes to get a promotion or to find other ways of breaking out of a job that has lost its challenge or its opportunities?

(5) Do I have enough self-assurance to take the risks or make sacrifices in order to retrain, move to another community, or take other steps that may be necessary to find a satisfying job in a particular field?

(6) Do I have the human relations skills that may be necessary for distinguished performance in a field that interests me?

(7) Would my job role interfere with my other roles (say, as mother or father) or with my moral and ethical values? Could I resolve such conflicts in a satisfactory manner?

(8) Do I know enough about how the use of power by management, unions, government, and other sectors of society affects the content of jobs and working conditions in various occupations?

(9) Am I able to draw information from history and the experience of others, or do I see a job and job problems as being unique and idiosyncratic?

When one reflects on only a few of the factors that relate to a person's job role, the importance of social studies in fortifying certain fundamental, job-related skills is clear.

Knowledge

The study of history gives perspective to Keith Goldhammer's concept of career education as "... a means of helping youngsters discover what their ultimate destiny in the world is."

The record of people living in past generations and varied cultures reveals the story of ordinary people whose lives revolved round what they did for a living. One can relate to their failures and their triumphs, and see these in the context of a social setting. In our own history, the student can relate to the people who worked at crafts or were small shopkeepers and can assess their work in relation to the status and needs of the society then and now. Learning about the work roles of floods of immigrants and immigrant-employer relations early in this century as well as learning about hazards in the mines, the exploitation of workers, the kinds of jobs in which women and children were employed, the turmoil and tragedy associated with early efforts to unionize, inventions that have altered industrial processes and consumer living standards, and the development of modern business and industry can all become part of a student's fund of knowledge about work. Understanding the impact of social change is useful to students in analyzing the effect that changing roles and organizations may have on their careers.

Economics can help the student understand the impact on the short- and long-term future of specific jobs that is caused by technological change, the availability of resources, supply and demand factors, changing consumer preferences, savings and investment, the relationship of the U.S. economy to foreign economies, and the federal government's monetary and fiscal policies.

Knowledge of sociology helps the student understand the effects that social class, ethnos, race, caste, and sex have had upon chances for entry and advancement in all kinds of jobs. Further, this knowledge provides insight into some of the personal adjustments that must be made when limitations imposed by social class or other factors are removed.

Knowledge of geography helps the student determine the availability and the long-term future of jobs in urban and rural areas, in various regions of the country, and in other parts of the world. Knowledge of political science helps build an understanding of how governmental policies can enhance or detract from the future of certain jobs in terms of income, attractiveness, permanence, number of job opportunities, and access to those jobs.

Values

The social sciences have become increasingly aware of the responsibility to give students tools with which to develop a set of values that will be satisfying to them and that, it is hoped, will strengthen our society at the same time. Many values are expressed, and often value conflicts experienced, in the course of selecting an occupation and carrying out work assignments. The Watergate tragedy has taught our generation how great an impact value systems can have on the entire social fabric as well as on individuals and their families.

The matter of life-style and the dedication one has to a particular life-style involve important choices among values. A high position in a prestigious profession may result from a quest for status rather than the pursuit of intellectual or managerial interests, and it may be the outgrowth of a value judgment made by one's parents. Often, the choices people make are well considered and fruitful, but sometimes value choices result in unhappy, unproductive, incompetent workers who are cut off from job roles that would give them greater satisfaction and that would have greater social benefit. Also, there are people who do not prepare for a professional or executive position, and subsequently yearn for it, who are equally unhappy.

Values clarification strategies in the social sciences do not impose a set of values on the student. Students are expected to do their own conscious selection of values through a careful study of alternatives and of the experiences other people have had. Generally, values selected in this manner will be well thought out. They will have given satisfaction to many people, and will have enlarged the contribution that people have made to their society, whether they worked as plumbers, carpenters, doctors, teachers' aides, printers, homemakers, or in some other occupation.

Attitudes

While there is a large body of evidence to support the view that most attitudes are established before a child enters school, there is also evidence that attitudes can be altered by the nature of a child's experience, including the school's instructional program. Attitudes toward work and level of performance, toward personal responsibility, and toward other people can be altered. Although for years social studies teachers have been concerned about attitudes in these areas, the tools and strategies for attitudinal change are of more recent origin.

Many attitudes that interfere with successful advancement in a career, it is now apparent, are based on myths or beliefs which at best are incomplete and at worst are totally erroneous. Among such attitudes are those in the human relations sector, where change involves coming to terms with one's feelings and opinions about people who differ from oneself. The observation of the anthropologist, the case studies of the sociologist, and the analytical studies of the political scientist — all transmitted in the school by the social studies teacher — are effective in freeing students of the myths and beliefs on which many old attitudes were based.

The current emphasis of the social studies on the richness and variety that racial, ethnic, religious, and cultural diversity bring to our society also has repercussions in the world of work. It is helping to alter attitudes that affect relations between workers and employers and to improve the quality of equal employment opportunity efforts.

Skills

Constructive attitudes in themselves do not necessarily produce good human relations, or improve a worker's abilities on the job. Skills are vital components of job success, and those taught in the social studies classroom have immediate and direct application to a student's career. Among these are the analytical skills that social scientists have developed to use in examining social edifices and human relationships. These skills can be applied to the selection of an occupation, and they frequently are significant in the quality of work performed by an individual in his or her job. Even in a depersonalized work atmosphere (such as an old-fashioned assembly line), the thoughtful and analytical worker often has been able to assess functional requirements in such a way that job improvements were made that resulted in savings to management, better working conditions, and an advancement for the innovative worker. In less structured work environments, such as that in sales or in small entrepreneurship, analytical skills commonly are indispensable to success on the job.

Human relations skills developed by the social sciences also have provided many specific tools used in employment. These tools have been used in human resource programs for the disadvantaged, in community programs for minority groups, and in personnel practices of large business organizations across the nation. Human relations skills not only can alter the character of the workplace but also provide job opportunities, such as employment counselor and community worker, which may have career interest for the social studies student.

Careers and Career Ladders

In addition to offering students these broad skills, social studies teachers also should infuse their teaching with an awareness of specific career possibilities for their students. Content in the social studies provides many springboards to develop career education units, and to relate subject matter to the career interests of students. Some of the changes in our society — among them, a steady increase in the proportion of workers in professional, technical, and service jobs and declines in agriculture, manufacturing, and transportation jobs — increase the likelihood that students will benefit in their careers from the social studies. Moreover, there are forecasts that shifts in the society's job needs will mean that students will have not a single career, but many different careers during their working lives. Consequently, most of them will benefit from a broad and flexible educational bakground in which social studies is a major component.

In helping students consider career possibilities, it may be useful to impress upon them the idea of career ladders. Many occupational areas offer opportunities for subprofessional employment, generally at the entry level, as well as formal educational or on-the-job training routes to higher paid jobs. There are, for example, career possibilities as teacher's aide, administrative trainee, nurse's aide, and legal aide, all of which can lead to further training and other work in the same general field. Also, the teacher should make students aware that careers related to the social studies tend to be far less subject to racist and sexist stereotyping than many other careers. Large numbers of minority group and women workers and professionals are found at every level in many of the social studies and related careers.

Following are some of the career fields directly related to social studies or in which a background of social studies makes a special contribution. Obviously, the list can be made far longer and would benefit by the addition of local employment opportunities. The career fields are listed in four categories: entry-level jobs, which usually involve no education after high school other than on-the-job training, and three categories which generally require additional formal education — generalized social studies and social science-related occupations, specialized jobs related mainly to a single social science discipline, and occupations indirectly related to social studies to which social studies has much to contribute.

Entry-Level Occupations

In this category, no formal education may be required after high school. Examples of entry-level occupations are:

Police officer	Firefighter
Postal clerk	Management trainee
Teacher's aide	Hospital aide
Social service aide	Library aide

Interdisciplinary Social Science Occupations

In the following sample occupations, college is usually required:

Social studies teacher	Marketing researcher
Urban planner	Government researcher
Educational administrator	Psychiatrist
Politician	Psychologist
Public administrator	Social studies textbook
Social studies curriculum	writer
specialist	Demographer
Social studies media	Lawyer
specialist	Judge
Foreign service officer	Accountant
Writer	

Specialized Social Science Occupations

In this category, college is required, although on rare occasions, some occupations have seen men and women who "came up through the ranks."

History

Teacher	Researcher
Writer	Museum curator
Administrator	Biographer
Archivist	Oral historian

Economics

Teacher	Business economist
Government economist	Agriculture economist

Writer
Investment counselor
Banker
Environmental economist

Labor economist
Stockbroker
Economic statistician

Political Science

Teacher
Government administrator
Writer

Politician
Researcher

Sociology

Teacher
Writer
Family worker
Criminologist

Researcher
Rural sociologist
Urban sociologist

Anthropology

Teacher
Ethnographer
Physical anthropologist
Social and cultural
   anthropologist

Archeologist
Ethnologist
Urban anthropologist
Writer

Geography

Teacher
Cartographer
Urban planner
Writer

Demographer
Urban biographer
Land use specialist

Careers Benefiting from Social Studies

Some careers in this fourth category require college. However, on-the-job training has proved effective in many instances. The first five occupations in the left-hand column are related to journalism.

Reporter
Columnist
Editor
Foreign correspondent
News analyst
Home economist

Internal revenue agent
Biographer
Public relations specialist
Conservation specialist
Business executive
Advertising copywriter

Architect	Insurance agent
Labor relations specialist	Personnel director
Camp director	Playground worker
Religious worker	Counselor
Government administrator	

Career Education's Contributions to Social Studies

The primary goal of the social studies teacher is to enhance the lifetime satisfactions and success of the student. Second, the teacher's goal is to improve the society through development of social awareness and understanding among its members. The tool for accomplishing these objectives is the social studies, and the first obligation of the social studies teacher is to teach social studies.

To contribute to career education, or anything else worthwhile, is admirable — so long as this does not interfere with the first obligation. Fortunately, there is no such conflict between career education and the teaching of social studies, but it is always desirable to keep priorities clear. The social studies can and should contribute to career education; it is more important to recognize that career education can contribute to social studies. This is the basic reason for using it.

As stated in a previous section, social studies not only contributes to career education, but there are mutual benefits as well. Career education offers the social studies motivation, illustration, and commitment.

Social studies is usually a popular class because its relevance to front-page news stories and television commentary is apparent to the alert student, who is "turned on" by increased understanding of the factors underlying current issues. Thus topical events are often used as a motivational device in the social studies classroom. But many students have not yet developed the self-assurance and maturity necessary to look beyond themselves at the broader society. They are too caught up in questions such as "Who am I?" and "Where do I fit into the scheme of things?" They are more likely to be motivated by evidence wherein the subject matter relates to them in concrete and immediate ways. Few secondary students are far removed from the question "What am I going to do with my life?" Subjects that can help them answer this question are most likely to catch their attention. Therefore, relating social studies to impending career choices can motivate students.

All youth are limited in exposure to the broad range of issues they confront in social studies class. Yet each has some understanding of the working world and how this can be related to the subject matter. Knowledge of the ways in which climate, terrain, and natural resources relate to what people do for a living in various parts of the world can help the teacher illustrate subject matter in geography. The causes of unemployment and shifts in the structure of employment by industry and occupation can illustrate the effects of economic policies. History can come alive around what common people have done to earn their sustenance. The home, the school, and the workplace are probably the most familiar settings to use in illustrating principles of human relations. The occupational world cannot and should not provide all of the illustrations needed to teach social studies, but it can provide many of them.

From motivation and illustration, commitment follows. If students are excited by a subject and understand it, enlightenment and success stimulate them, and more intellectual intoxication is desired and sought. Anyone now happy in a career probably recalls this process by indulging in retrospection. And what is more exciting to a teacher than to have a student become so interested in a course that it becomes the basis for a career choice?

Instructional Strategies

How does a teacher introduce career education into a classroom? Obviously, the teacher cannot do this alone. School administrators, supervisors, and teachers all should be involved in orientation meetings and workshops to learn the relationship between social studies and career education and to establish the specific responsibilities of all concerned for introducing this material into the social studies curriculum.

Career education should not be "added on" to social studies courses. It should be fused into courses in such a way that students can see the relationships between the subjects they study and the world of work. This requires the development of a carefully designed plan, based on an analysis of each course component, and decisions as to where fusion is suitable and how it is to be achieved.

Teachers should have time to review existing course content in order to identify relevant career opportunities and to ready plans which will enable students to explore the character of various occupations. A career education coordinator might be used to help the teacher develop these plans. Also, community resources should be identified during the planning process. It may be useful during this stage to enlist people outside the school system as planning consultants who can explain the operation of various businesses, point out existing and future job opportunities, and identify the various kinds of skills needed in different jobs. Later, the same resources can be drawn upon to give students direct contacts with the world of work.

New materials that might be used in the classroom should be examined. Some of these, such as simulations and games about employment, can be helpful in giving students safe ways to experience aspects of work without the fear of making errors that might be damaging in real life situations. Furthermore, these materials can open new horizons and offer students insights into potential careers they may never have considered. Many of the new instructional materials of this kind have been put together so that the competent teacher can use them with little or no special instruction.

When social studies plans for career education are made, it is important that they cover the development of broad student skills as well as the acquisition of detailed career information. In order to evaluate their career opportunities, students must be able to clarify their values, use research and evaluation techniques — observing, reading, interviewing, comparing, contrasting, categorizing, and generalizing — and make judgments based on what they learn about an occupation in relation to what they know about themselves.

Goals for Career Education Planning

In shaping plans for the social studies classroom, a teacher must establish the goals for infusing classroom work with career education. Any single list of goals may have to be adapted to meet the needs of a particular school, social studies department, or teacher. But in general the goals that are selected should make it possible for students to:

(1) Develop positive self-concepts

(2) Develop attitudes and cognitive skills for successful and continued employment

(3) Learn the importance of making wise choices by sharing in decision making on matters that affect their school life, such as curriculum, course goals and objectives, kinds of learning activities, evaluation procedures, and school activities outside the classroom

(4) Relate subject content and learning activities to occupations that directly and indirectly benefit from a knowledge of social studies

(5) Be exposed to workers and occupations representing a wide range of job levels, from unskilled to professional

(6) Meet people working in social science and related occupations and have an opportunity to learn from these persons about the nature of their work

(7) Learn how to use various media and other resources in order to acquire information about educational and training requirements for entry-level jobs and employment at higher pay in other fields, the working conditions in these occupations, and the economic implications of careers in which they are interested

(8) Be involved in exploring career situations through such means as role playing

(9) Learn the effect that certain occupations have on leisure time activities, civic participation, family responsibilities, and moral and ethical beliefs and values

(10) Have opportunities for paid or unpaid jobs in career interest areas

(11) Realistically shape tentative career plans

Using Classroom Opportunities

To meet these goals, a teacher can use a number of strategies to make career education a vital element in the social studies classroom. The organization and function of the class itself offers many opportunities for the development of such lifelong skills as decision making, inquiry, and self-direction. To make maximum use of these opportunities, the teacher should alter the traditional role. Teachers who are comfortable in the role of facilitator, consultant, and guide will allow their students to experience the establishment of purposes for a social studies course and to set specific performance objectives, learning activities, and evaluation procedures. Others may have difficulty doing so and should seek alternative ways to reach the same general goals.

In most cases, the best way to help youth gain a better understanding of themselves, perceive their potential, and understand their work opportunities is to draw information from a subject area and extend it to include related careers, thus helping students examine many life-styles and relate them to specific occupations. Discussions about personal, group, and societal values can help students make decisions. Also, a closer look at occupations in which social studies information is a necessary component can enrich student understanding of relationships between what is learned in school and the world outside the school. This broadening of the social studies will require that some time be set aside in the classroom for students to explore careers. In the following paragraphs, some ways that teachers can plan career-related experiences, in the context of existing social studies programs, are presented.

History

One topic taught in history courses that can be related to career evaluation is technological change. From studying early history, the teacher can find simple forms of technological invention to serve as springboards for studying career implications — tools for gathering and producing food, the wheel, fire, and writing. Inventions appearing after the tenth century — the modern form of the clock, the printing press, the factory system, the ball-point pen, automatic weapons, the telephone, and the computer — can be used to continue student awareness of careers. Students can examine the effects of these inventions on people's working lives and explore how such inventions terminated certain kinds of jobs and created other kinds. Lessons or student projects could be developed to guide student study of an undustry, of job clusters, of specific occupations, of career change over a period of years, of social implications, and of cross-cultural implications. The same approach can be used with history topics such as:

Topic	Application
Agricultural revolution	Food-related functions: growing, processing, packaging, distributing, preparing, wholesaling, jobbing, warehousing, retailing, and dietetic careers
Emergence of complex living patterns	Urban planning, development, and rehabilitation; trade; social work, occupational training; government administration careers
Epidemics and catastrophes	Health, land use and restoration, fire protection, law enforcement, and social service careers
Ethnic studies	Teaching; esthetic careers in writing, art, and music
Exploration and colonization	Space exploration, marine science, aerospace industries, trade, international economic development careers
Lives of people	Biographer, leadership training, administration, management, human service, research, invention
Preservation of artifacts, architecture, institutions, and values	Archeologist, anthropologist, architect, designer, planner, museum work
State history	Careers related to the geography, economics, and culture of the state
Use of scientific tools to study the human experience	Careers in historical study and analysis
Wars	Weapons and ordnance manufacture, distribution, and acquisition; Armed Forces and military education careers

Sample Exercise — United States history: "Wild West"

This sample exercise shows how a single topic in a U.S. history course can be adapted to career education concepts. The primary career cluster assignments to be emphasized are public service careers.

a) Identify the common career goals that apply to this course.

b) Establish and write specific objectives to show what career cluster information and experiences are sought. (This should be done for each goal listed.) The objectives might be to have students select, explore, and work in an occupational setting to find: work activities and responsibilities; salary potential and fringe benefits; congruency with aptitudes, abilities, interests, values, and anticipated life-styles; employment opportunities and potential for advancement; education and skills requirements; nature of the work (seasonal, regional, hazardous, working with people); and the like.

c) List specific student experiences to reach these goals:

1) Identify the occupations of immigrants in the Old West and compare them to the occupations of people in the modern-day West.

2) Compare the role and responsibilities of the "Indian agent" during the Wild West period with those of the government worker on today's Indian reservations.

3) Compare the role and responsibilities of marshals, deputies, and sheriffs in those days with today's law enforcement officers.

4) Analyze the relationship of settlers in the early West to the environment, recognizing that an abundance of natural resources tended to encourage waste and that what students see in movie houses and on television today is not necessarily "the way it was." Identify the resulting problems and attitudes today.

5) Role play a town meeting at which the problem of law and order is being considered: A man has been accused of a brutal murder and thrown in jail. Several people in the town have differing and conflicting views about what should be done. Roles to be played include: sheriff, judge, mayor, arresting deputy, victim's relatives, prisoner, prisoner's relatives, persons in favor of lynching, and those against. Follow with a discussion of why a trial should be held and why early Westerners sometimes took the law into their own hands, and a discussion of mob behavior.

d) List resource needs — materials, people, field trips, or other items necessary to reach the goals of this course.

e) Evaluate the course by deciding how well it met its objectives.

Geography

Modern geography courses have advanced beyond the "place" geography that was once taught. Today, geography studies aid students in developing thinking skills and in associating ideas. The study of a region, for example, provides many opportunities to examine spatial interaction and areal association. This can be an excellent starting point for a social studies teacher to introduce career implications of subject content. In the urban region, interesting career opportunities have emerged in urban planning, land use and resource allocation, building inspection and rehabilitation, and mass transportation. Many students could reinforce their understanding of geographic concepts while actively learning more about careers in these fields. The career implications of other topics in geography could be:

Topic	Application
Adaptation to the environment	Soil management and land use careers
Economic geography	Geographer doing plant site study and analysis, international business
Energy	Energy exploration, production, and management
Physical surface of the earth	Geologist, geographer, weather researcher, and announcer
Population	Demographer, population planner
Urbanization	Urban planning, development, and rehabilitation

Economics

The teaching of economics offers many opportunities to stimulate career exploration by students. For example, a significant topic in many economics courses is the concept of scarcity, followed by the allocation of limited resources. Students exploring this topic learn of the relationship between economic decisions that individuals and society make and how these decisions affect the distribution of limited resources in the economic system. Whatever these resources, avenues for career exploration are available.

Scarcity of iron ore and its allocation could lead to the study of careers in the steel and mining industries and in those industries that produce metals that might serve as substitutes for iron and steel.

A shortage of doctors — with its consequent allocation of medical services — could lead to a study of the social and economic implications of health maintenance organizations, and then to a study of the career opportunities in health-care professions. Career implications of other topics in economics are suggested as follows:

Topic	Application
Capital goods	Machine tools careers, product management, financial careers
Distribution	Transportation careers
Divisions of labor	Labor union careers, business management careers
Employment	Employment agencies, social service, personal careers
Input-output	Economists, data processing careers
Personal and consumer economics	Small business, consumer protection, governmental service careers
Productivity	Engineering, systems analyses, supervisory careers
Savings and investment	Banking, security, and investment careers; insurance; accounting careers
Supply and demand	Wholesaling and retailing careers
Trade and interdependence	Import-export careers

Political Science

Civics, government, and political science courses contain a number of concepts useful in developing career interests. For example, the concept of law — the fact that every society has laws or rules that govern the conduct of its human behavior — is common in political science. This concept enables the teacher to offer learning experiences that open the eyes of students to a great many careers, including those in law-making structures at local, county, state, and federal levels, in legislative support, and lobbying. A number of other political science topics and their suggested career applications are:

Topic	Application
Citizenship and the political process	Political party careers, lobbying, and government service careers

Enforcement of laws	Law enforcement careers
International organizations	Trade, cultural exchange, and government careers
Interpretation of laws	Court-related careers
National goals	Government-related careers

Sociology and Anthropology

Human behavior in groups and institutions is a concern of these two broad areas. However, abstract normative or functional concepts often are studied in social studies classes without revealing ways that students can gain even an elementary awareness of career opportunities related to the concepts that are presented.

One example of how relatively abstract concepts in these subjects can be more readily understood in terms of careers is in the study of social and technological change. If a teacher introduces the concept of automation through discussion of the invention of the computer, there is a good opportunity to analyze resulting social changes and career implications. Other possible uses of sociology and anthropology topics in career education are:

Topic	Application
Conflict	Crisis intervention careers
Family	Family counseling careers
Human relationships	Child development, education, personnel, psychology careers
Leisure	Recreation, social service, planning careers
Racism	Race relations, teaching careers
Religion	Religious careers
Sexism	Human development, education, and antidiscrimination enforcement careers
Social structure	Organizational structure, analysis, consulting careers

Philosophy and Psychology

Although courses in philosophy and psychology are not offered universally, many schools now provide mini-courses or units in these fields. Teachers have an excellent opportunity to develop student interest in the improvement of the human condition through human service occupations if career implications are studied when topics such as interpersonal and intergroup relationships are discussed. Concepts of these relationships involve the study of conflict and conflict resolution (coping) skills. Careers in human relations, counseling, and psychiatric treatment are natural avenues for career exploration that can accompany the study of these concepts in a philosophy or psychology course or unit.

In a philosophy course or unit, the study of the human search for meaning in life also offers an opportunity to bring career education into the classroom. Other examples of the way that philosophy and psychology topics can be related to career education are:

Topic	*Application*
Attitudes and values	Psychology, education, philosophy, religious careers
Death	Funeral service, medical, religious careers
Learning and training	Teaching, testing, personnel development careers
Mental health and illness	Psychology, health careers
Religion	Religious education and religious careers
Self-development	Counseling, teaching, psychology careers

Interdisciplinary Studies

Although many of the social science disciplines that have been discussed imply interdisciplinary relationships, there are other possibilities for career education in social science courses that concentrate on human problems, such as environmental considerations, poverty, crime, intergroup conflicts, and peace. All of these courses offer the opportunity to inquire into careers that are emerging in these areas. For example, a course on environmental problems can create awareness of career implications in such sectors as environmental health, problem detection, regulation, and law enforcement. Information skills in this area — interviewing, research, writing, and information retrieval — offer other career possibilities.

Using Outside Resources

It is clear that one way social studies can be made far more relevant to students is by giving students firsthand familiarity with related careers. Getting to know people whose jobs are enhanced in some way by a knowledge of social studies content and a mastery of social studies skills adds the dimension of many human responses to what otherwise might be a collection of dull facts.

The vast array of business, organizations, and institutions in a community can be used to excellent advantage. A school district or an individual school can organize a school-community with major responsibilities for exploring ways of shaping a partnership between the school and the world of work. This committee could propose and expedite many opportunities for school administrators, teachers, students, and parents to learn about the requirements, responsibilities, roles, values, and needs in different occupations.

For example, the committee might sponsor a career education workshop for students at which working men and women would describe occupations in their particular fields and answer student questions about their jobs. The workshops might include demonstrations of specific occupations, such as tailoring, hairdressing, small motor repair, drafting, and others. Visits to businesses, sponsored by the school-community committee, would enable students to see occupations in a natural setting. Members of the local police department, for example, might invite some students to visit police headquarters, where students could get an insider's view of various careers — and stages of careers — in law enforcement. The broad knowledge now required in this field may surprise some students if their image of police work is largely one of guns and sirens.

A visit to the office of city planners to discuss their work will help students learn about the complex issues that planners deal with and something of how they go about their jobs. A visit to a large business or public institution for a vertical look at employment — from entry-level to top management — can clarify how each worker contributes to the operation and can give students an overall picture of how a large business functions. Later, students could explore in the classroom the role that business plays in the economic life of the community.

Trips to a cluster of related businesses could give another type of perspective. If students are studying the role of communications, for example, trips to the various media (radio, television, newspaper, magazines, and the visual and performing arts) can give them clues into the myriad ways that people communicate ideas. These trips can demonstrate the great array of jobs in each field, as well as the similarities and differences among jobs in different, but related, fields.

After-school or summer jobs in the community also can open avenues for career thought. For many students, such jobs are an economic necessity and may be the first step into adult careers. However, students who can afford to work as volunteers may find it worthwhile simply to learn about all of the opportunities there are to participate in the life of the community. Student internship in political organizations, for example, can stimulate interest in the voting process, and lead to better understanding of the need for individual participation in government. Moreover, this work can help students learn about the skills and information politicians need to hold their jobs.

Evaluating Results

The appraisal of individual student capabilities, interests, and needs should be done several times during the year. In making these assessments, attention should be given to the skills and knowledge in occupations related to the social studies as well as in those that traditionally have been the responsibility of the social studies.

Several kinds of evaluative instruments, formal and informal, and various procedures can be used to advantage. In psychology and other behavioral science classes, pre- and posttest interest, aptitude, and attitude tests can be given if the teacher is qualified to administer and interpret the tests to each student. In any case, the classroom teacher and the school counselor can work as a team to help students make realistic decisions, based on such tests, plus achievement and intelligence tests.

In social studies classes outside the behavioral sciences, evaluation items can be developed from the specific performance objectives for each course. This assumes that an adequate number of realistic performance objectives has been established.

Simple questionnaires, developed by teachers or by teachers and students working together, can help students make self-assessments. These questionnaires also can help teachers plan what to emphasize in class content and can help them devise instructional strategies to meet student needs. Questionnaires can relate to a specific topic, such as "Individual Mastery of

Skills." In this type of instrument, one item might be: How well do I make up questions for interviews? Students would evaluate their performance in terms of "poor," "good," or "very good." The students should be encouraged to keep personal data notebooks, to be added to each year, so that their personality profiles will be substantially accurate and consequently more useful.

A number of professionally developed inventories, designed to help teachers and students get at personal characteristics, are on the market. In addition, the professional literature contains informal instruments that can be used with the permission of the author. Of course, the ultimate measure of success for a career education program is the proportion of students who attain personal fulfillment, and this cannot be determined while students are still in school.

Selected References

Bailey, Larry; and Stadt, Ronald. *Career Education: New Approaches to Human Development.* Bloomington, Illinois: McKnight & McKnight Publishing Company. 1973.

Bolles, Richard. *What Color Is Your Parachute? A Practical Manual for Job Hunters and Career Changers.* New York: Crown Publishers, Inc. 1972.

Cook, Iva Dean. *Occupational Notebook.* Champaign, Illinois: Research Press. 1972.

Darcy, Robert; and Powell, Phillip. *Manpower and Economic Education.* Denver: Love Publishing Co. 1973.

Goldhammer, Keith; and Taylor, Robert. *Career Education: Perspective and Promise.* Columbus, Ohio: Charles E. Merrill Books, Inc. 1972.

Hoyt, Kenneth B.; *et al. Career Education: What It Is and How to Do It.* Second edition. Salt Lake City: Olympus Publishing Company. 1974.

Liston, Robert. *On-the-Job Training and Where to Get It.* New York: Julian Messner, Inc. 1973.

McClure, Larry; and Buan, Carolyn. Editors. *Essays on Career Education.* Portland, Oregon: Northwest Regional Educational Laboratory. 1973.

Ober, Keith; and Kearins, Kathryn. *Exploring Careers.* Cambridge: Abt Associates, Inc. 1973.

Ohio Department of Education. *Career Orientation Program.* Columbus: Ohio Department of Education. 1973.

Simon, Sidney; *et al. Values Clarification.* New York: Hart Publishing Co. 1972.

Splaver, Sarah. *Your Career If You're Not Going to College.* New York: Julian Messner, Inc. 1971.

Terkel, Studs. *Working.* New York: Pantheon Books. 1974.

U.S. Department of Labor. *Occupational Outlook Handbook.* Washington, D.C.: U.S. Department of Labor. 1974.

6
The Visual Arts and Career Education

National Art Education Association

John J. Mahlmann
National Art Education Association
Reston, Virginia

Charles M. Dorn
Purdue University
West Lafayette, Indiana

Leroy Gaskin
North Englewood, Maryland

Stanley Madeja
University City, Missouri

Ann Richardson
School Board of Charles County
La Plata, Maryland

6
Career Education
in the Visual Arts Classroom

To the art educator, art is a means to an end as well as an end in itself. Its forms, its creations, and its perceptions enrich the lives of all humans, whether they make their living in the arts or in other fields. At the same time, art constitutes an end in itself not only for artists but for people in a large number of occupations whose work calls for some art knowledge.

Art instruction in secondary schools generally has three major components: (1) the development of perception, understanding, and appreciation, (2) a study of art history and of art criticism and analysis, and (3) production. These are interwoven studies. The history and analysis component, for example, deals with the relevance of art in different periods, and this in turn not only adds to the students' cognitive knowledge but enhances their appreciation of such elements as line, form, color, and design.

Running like a strong thread through all art instruction in secondary schools is the idea that human responses are built from feelings and emotions as well as from facts and information, and that there are flexible, creative, and emotional responses which are uniquely human. As a result, art instructors try to develop in students not only cognitive understanding and specific skills but also their sensory, appreciative, and creative abilities to use in all aspects of their lives.

105

Beyond developing esthetic appreciation (an important but fairly well-understood function of art), what can art add to the education of most students? Is art production by students who will become computer specialists, for example, an activity that has only recreational potential for them? Actually, art production has many elements that have great relevance and value in the work aspects of most people's lives. This is because it requires the manipulation of materials and forms, the organization of ideas, and creative approaches to new kinds of problems. What is produced is not just art that can be seen or heard but also many skills — composed of sensitivities, human understanding, and complex and creative problem-solving strategies — that are indispensable in trade and industry, international affairs, and personal relationships, as well as in the various professional art fields.

Art also helps people find satisfaction in whatever work they do. The future mechanic learns through the study of art to appreciate the tools and the tasks of the trade on an esthetic level. The future forester can learn to see all elements of the forest, great and small, as well as the trees. The budding computer programmer can develop a pleasurable awareness of the visual patterns of the machines, of the ordered data, and of sound and movement in a computer center. To everyday tasks, art adds a meaningful human dimension to the functional requirements and satisfactions of jobs and helps make work of all kinds more meaningful to the worker. All careers, whether routine or constantly in flux, can be more meaningful to the individual in that abstract, but truly real way, in which participation in the environment is appreciated on the level of the senses, emotions, and feelings.

But even though these contributions of art education are well recognized in principle, the art educator in practice often is subject to a general field bias and is strongly committed to the idea of art for its own sake. Standing on this ground, teachers often feel they can better maintain the integrity of their discipline, serve students who are talented in art, and resist pressures — some of them imaginary, some of them real — to restructure art programs into mere training activities for future sign painters, window dressers, or decorators for local department stores. Because art classes are universally an elective, whereas other academic courses are required, the art teacher can succeed in attracting or repelling a large segment of the student body with the approach taken to art instruction. Serving large numbers of students well calls for a recognition of the many opportunities for career involvement that exist in art. Yet some art may not necessarily be produced by the fine artist, but the same methods and principles of work are embodied in its production. It is particularly in this area that career education can make a major contribution to widening the demand for art instruction in secondary schools.

The purpose of career education is not to put students in some ready-made occupational slots, such as sign painter, and then train them so that they fit. Rather, the thrust of career education is wide, interdisciplinary, and responsive to a broad band of student needs — many of them, simply human needs — that impinge upon the occupational aspects of their lives. The goal of career education is to help all students prepare for a meaningful and satisfying life and livelihood as adults. It does this by helping them become conscious of their own values and options; explore the world of work and themselves in relation to it; develop judgmental, decision-making, and organizational skills; and help them prepare for specific careers in broad, functional ways so that as occupational requirements change or as they change, they can continue to respond successfully. This is a major undertaking, and it requires that there be no little slots or boxes to place students in but that every element of the school system be employed in an effort to prepare all students to lead well-rounded lives.

Building meaningful programs which will identify important relationships between the study and creation of art with the world of work and its vast occupational potentials demands that the teacher may have to alter any traditional field biases that are present in the classroom. While the general field bias toward art for its own sake, which tends to separate even college programs into distinct tracts, may remain as a personal commitment on the part of the teacher, it is inappropriate for most adolescents in secondary school art programs. It is the responsibility of the art teacher to help students identify the values and benefits of other approaches to the use of art as well as those in art for its own sake. Then, students can decide for themselves the directions in which they will go. This general, open approach usually is favored even in the beginning stages of art training at higher education levels.

The nature of the art discipline implies that individuals and their personal expression are an integral part of the subject matter. This content affects how the career opportunities in art are addressed and how they can be translated into occupational categories. Often, the personal choice for a career in art is one based on an inverse ratio between the amount of individual freedom — or creative expression — the individual needs vs job security and income. Dorn, Hansen, and Madeja, in their essay "The Arts and Work," said that in choosing a career direction in art, the individual's attitude toward individual freedom is important:

> If the individual considers that it is important to have a great deal of freedom, he may sacrifice the security of wages and income. This is not to say, however, that a prominent artist in any of the arts is not compensated well for his services; on the contrary, chances of rewards are very great both monetarily and in status. There is, however, a continuum of occupational choices in the arts based on personal satisfaction. If the occupation demands maximum audience acceptance, the degrees of personal freedom are reduced considerably, whereas if in the occupation you are only responsible to yourself to produce or create works of art, then the degrees of freedom are greater and audience acceptance needs are much less. For example, if one chooses to be a poet, a creative writer, a sculptor, a painter, or a composer of music, a great deal of freedom and personal reward is offered to the individual; however, the guarantee of a consistent wage per year is not as likely.... If an occupation such as designer or lighting technician is chosen, the chances of a more stable income and position are greater. A designer, say in the auto industry, has another problem — that of a mass audience to appeal to; therefore his designs must be dictated to some extent by this audience.... The poet has only himself to satisfy, and he takes a chance whether or not the audience accepts it. The auto designer is not "successful" if he does not obtain large audience acceptance. The poet

may receive rejection instantly by a large audience but over time gain a lasting reputation.

There are of course many variations that occur. There are graphic designers who work in a design studio and are assigned tasks, and there are free-lance designers who initiate their own projects and accept only design problems that are akin to their philosophy. There are painters who work without knowing whether they will be able to sell their paintings, and there are those who function much the same as Velásquez who worked as a court painter on subjects selected by his employer.

An important factor in occupational choice in art is talent. Art has been consistently a subject matter only for the talented, with limited participation by others who are not gifted in this area. But especially as it relates to occupational choices, the idiom that the artist is born and that art is not learned is suspect. Art can be learned, as can the ability to perceive as an artist perceives. Obviously, natural talent helps to achieve success in art. Someone highly talented in drawing is likely to be a better illustrator, or to become one with less effort, than one who is not. But talent should not be the only criterion used in determining whether students should pursue careers in art, nor should it limit those who might enter allied occupations in which art knowledge and training are useful.

Along with recognizing, encouraging, and developing students who are likely to become professional artists, the art instructor must identify ways to help other students mesh their art education with their career education needs. For these students — and they are by far the majority in the art classroom — the teacher needs to make the art discipline relevant to the individual both through vocational opportunities and through many specific applications to all areas of human endeavor. By doing so, the teacher helps students make a transition from the abstract, the mystical, and the intangible qualities of art to relevant and meaningful personal applications in the world in which most of them will work. This not only makes art of interest to students who otherwise might not have participated in it, it enhances the value of art in their educational development and in society.

Questions about what is to be taught become important when the teacher starts to design classroom activities for career education in art. It should be helpful at this point to examine the U.S. Office of Education's fifteen career clusters. These clusters meet four basic requirements: (1) they encompass all types of jobs in the Labor Department's *Dictionary of Occupational Titles*, (2) they include jobs at all levels, (3) they relate to identifiable groups of employers, and (4) they are recurring over time. Art falls in the "fine arts and humanities" cluster. Within this unit, the fine arts are subdivided into seven areas, each with its own typical occupations:

(1) Creating

    (a) Painting

    (b) Printmaking

    (c) Sculpture

    (d) Musical composition

(2) Performing

    (a) Dance

    (b) Dramatic arts

    (c) Music

    (d) Films, radio, television

(3) Performing arts design

    (a) Stage set design

    (b) Stage lighting design

    (c) Costume design

(4) Performing arts production

    (a) Stage set construction

    (b) Stage lighting

    (c) Costume production

    (d) Stage equipment

(5) Artist management

    (a) Human relations (performing and nonperforming)

    (b) Public relations

(6) Visual and graphics design

  (a) Illustration

  (b) Industrial design

  (c) Fashion design

  (d) Environmental design

(7) Media

  (a) Fim and tape editing

  (b) Film processing

  (c) Camera and recording operation

When a program to identify cogent relationships between classroom activities and the world of work is conceptualized, there are a number of things the art teacher should keep in mind. First, an attempt to present the information, concepts, and experiences relevant to careers in art implies some engagement or simulation of the occupation in classroom activity. But it does not require that preprofessional training in the occupation should take place. In fact, even at the advanced levels of training offered in art schools or universities, the instructors often avoid specific work applications in favor of teaching concepts that will provide insights on how to solve a multitude of specific job-related tasks. Moreover, the teacher should recognize the limitations of the secondary school classroom in preparing students to enter many of the technical and highly skilled art occupations. There are fields which require artists to undergo very strenuous and highly technical training over a long period of time, often as much as six to eight years of professional preparation in a specific area. The art teacher should also keep in mind the fact that there can be direct carry-over from one field to another — for example, the visual artist who specializes in printmaking is likely to know about commercial printing and photographic techniques as well as the traditional techniques used in lithography, serigraphy, etching, and engraving.

What is needed in career education in art is not vocational education for art jobs. Indeed the most effective program probably will emphasize the broad functions underlying success in a wide variety of occupations, rather than emphasizing all possible art-related occupations and the specific art skills each one requires. The cluster approach, while useful in determining the kinds of jobs available in the art field may not be so useful in the classroom as would be the categorization of art careers by occupational functions. In the visual arts, for example, there are many differences among them in the nature of the art form produced, but in a world-of-work sense, they also have some striking similarities. For example, craftworkers, artisans, and people who work as fine artists perform many similar functions. Though these functions are not identical in all visual arts fields, or always permit immediate transfer, the functions are more alike than different.

Analyzing Art Careers by Function

The functions that apply to the visual arts generally can be described as creative, re-creative, managerial, technically supportive, and consumer related. These five functions can be further delineated as:

(1) *Creative art:* Generally applies to positions such as painter, printmaker, sculptor, or craftworker in which there is a relatively high degree of freedom. Some in this category create works of art solely for artistic results. There are others — architects and industrial, graphics, and interior designers — who must work to a client's specifications and may have to collaborate with workers and management from other disciplines in order to do their work.

(2) *Re-creative art:* Covers activities that require a high degree of skills in producing prototypes and multiple reproductions of an artist's concept or model. Included are production potters, jewelers, printing press operators, foundry workers, and others who have extensive skills and sensitivity to works of art but whose jobs do not require the creation of original work. (Creative artists sometimes perform the re-creative function, making copies of their own work.)

(3) *Art management:* Requires an organizing or collating function but essentially managerial in character. These

positions include museum, art, and dance directors, production coordinators, film producers, and design coordinators. Often these positions require the individual to work under the supervision of a sculptor, architect, designer, or other creative artist in performing a function that is largely organizational and supportive. The skills required may be in the area of business or financial support. At other times, these positions call for highly creative skills (organizing major art shows, for example), and in such cases the individual may need thorough knowledge of the art.

(4) *Technical support:* Probably the function with the largest number of positions in the arts which require special expertise and training in one or more aspects of an art form. In this general category are jobs such as printer, foundry worker, draftsman or draftswoman, and photographer. These people usually are highly skilled and may work under the direction of a manager, or in some cases directly with an individual performer. The positions often do not require that the person be familiar with a total operation or be responsible for the final execution of a performance or craft.

(5) *Consumer-related functions:* Least common of all positions in the arts. In this category are persons who serve as critics, reviewers, editors, and curators. Generally they make their living by writing, philosophizing, collecting, or selling in the many occupational fields of the arts. Normally such persons must have broad expertise in a specific art and must have been trained for specialized literary or curatorial capabilities.

It is evident that in the arts there are many educational opportunities which vary from those that are individualistic in nature to those that are tied closely to various segments of industry. Many jobs and many job functions are applicable to more than one art area. Moreover, occupations in art are constantly changing. There is renewed interest, for example, in handmade goods which are produced in limited quantities and designed by good craftworkers. Modern technologies are also opening up many new jobs for artists.

Various approaches to teaching the arts offer different options. If a unit of study is specifically job centered, it may be limited to a few career discussions. If it involves many fields and many levels of activity, it will provide a wide range of careers for examination. Optimum use of the potential for career discussion that is inherent in art requires the exploration of all available options.

Furthermore, while recognition is given to occupations in art and its allied fields, the uses of art in nearly all occupations — in helping a mechanic or a forester be creative, to see facets of work that otherwise might not be seen, to shape ideas into problem-solving patterns, and so forth — should *not* be neglected. Teachers of the arts must serve not only extremely creative and talented students — and those who come into the classroom bearing some special kinds of technical proclivities — but also a large student population that is earnestly seeking "to become." These students seek personal, work, and other societal roles and too often are shunted aside. Serving a large student group means that the art instructor must not simply point out strongly art-oriented occupations that some students may enter, but also the practicable uses of art in all occupations.

Classroom Strategies for Career Education

This section is devoted to giving strategies that a teacher could employ in the classroom to guide students in their exploration of careers in the arts. Units are designed to demonstrate teaching methods that use some current curriculum approaches and involve awareness of specific careers, exploration of potential careers, and hands-on experiential knowledge of careers.

Class projects may lead to awareness of careers through content concerning the artist, designer, or architect who produces work in the area studied. In addition to studying art forms, the student should learn about individual artists and the role of the artist in society.

Students can practice a career in the classroom through simulation of specific functions. By doing so, the student learns more about the career role involved. If the media or some other broad area is the basis for the unit, students might observe and try out a variety of roles.

Unit One   *Specific Careers*   *Related Careers*
Architect   Highway designer
Urban planner   Environmentalist
Landscape architect
Public planner
Politician

Architecture and urban planning have many career implications, and a wide variety of art functions can be covered in this unit. Highway design, public facilities planning, landscape design, and environmental considerations, for example, are all part of the work of urban planners. By studying the broadest concepts of architecture and urban planning, students can discuss a number of careers. After all, the functions involved in an area as complex as urban development cover an enormous range, from the architect who is a creator to the manager and, finally, to the consumer and the critic.

At the awareness level, the art class might study visuals of architecture — shopping plazas, city design, and highway projections. Further exploration would include the history of urban planning and architectural design and facts about individual designers and architects. Hands-on experience might include planning and constructing an architectural model, planning a shopping center, and designing a campus or a section of a city. Field trips to architectural firms and to architectural sites and important buildings might be components of the project. Community resources should be explored to emphasize the social aspects of urban development and the related work that politicians do.

Unit Two   *Specific Careers*   *Related Careers*
Systems designer   Application in the fields
Product designer   of each design, from
Graphic designer   simple implements to
complex machines (the
automobile or jet
aircraft)

As part of the design project, students might redesign everyday objects. The product designer, students will learn, has the function of creator, is sensitive to the needs of society, and must satisfy the consumer. Student awareness can be stimulated by selection of the product to be redesigned. Looking at products is the beginning of design considerations. Redesigning a doorknob, a toaster, a tape player, or a service cart leads to knowledge of the designer's function. Outstanding studios and designers should be studied, such as Charles Eames, Herman Miller, and Bauhaus. Products should be discussed in functional and esthetic terms, and students can construct models of projected designs.

Unit Three	*Specific Careers*	*Related Careers*
	Theater designer	Set designer
	Actor	Audio expert
	Filmmaker	Lighting expert
	Photographer	Costume designer
	Producer-director	Animator
	Television writer	Makeup artist
		Prompter
		Musician

Filmmaking, a synthetic art form, offers many areas for career consideration. Awareness begins with the viewing and discussion of selected films in terms of art, film history, and filming techniques. Printed materials on these subjects also encourage further exploration. Production of a film teaches the student to identify all of the roles needed for the production.

The organization and cooperative efforts needed to produce a film would allow students to observe many related career options beyond those listed above. And they would see the manner in which workers relate to one another. Field trips to a film or television studio might be part of the class study of filmmaking careers. Resource people, in talking to students, may be helpful in suggesting other specialties, such as the artist who creates backgrounds for film animation or the courtroom artist who does drawings of the judge, defendant, and jury when cameras are not permitted in the courtroom.

Students who are seeking some degree of team activity and the satisfaction of group achievement in an arts environment may want to consider options provided by this unit. The functional range in filmmaking is broad and covers many interests, including as it does the creative, re-creative, management, technical support, and critical functions.

Unit Four	*Specific Careers*	*Related Careers*
	Painter	Fabric design
	Interior designer	Printmaking
	Textile designer	Optics
	Printer	Serigraphy
	Optician	Graphic artist
	Fashion designer	Photographer

An established classroom unit of study on painting and color offers many career options. This unit may be part of an advanced painting project or part of a basic design course. The experience of using color and light to produce a painting enables a student to explore the career of a painter. Study concerning the role of the painter and his or her expression and techniques is essential to understanding the art of painting. Slides and reproductions of paintings can also provide an awareness of the art form and its functions. Visits to galleries and art studios to see art and artists firsthand are desirable.

Class discussion of painting as a career might include the value of this career to the individual and to society, and the attitudes that society displays toward the painter. The discussion should also cover related career possibilities. While the painter is a creator who works in terms of idiosyncratic expression, there are many similar careers that involve other functions. Students should be encouraged to identify alternate career selections which are similar in terms of skills, esthetics, and background knowledge. Linking the painter's career with these other careers allows the students to decide which area might be most appropriate for his or her further investigation.

Students who do not want careers in art are often interested in printing and its allied fields (such as printmaking) as re-creational activities. For them, art expands the boundaries of other careers by offering ways to achieve individual expression and a high degree of personal satisfaction.

Unit Five

Specific Careers	*Related Careers*
Exhibit designer	Management
Graphic designer	Exhibitor
Illustrator	Layout design
Cartoonist	Color coordinator
Display artist	
Scenic designer	

These careers offer many satisfactions in discovering and working out solutions to visual communications problems. However, these career roles might not be evident in a studio art course. It may be necessary to engage in interdisciplinary activities with the school to define the various career roles in this unit. These activities might include displays, bulletin boards, exhibits, and showcases. In addition, there may be many areas in the school where the art department could enhance the environment. These might include courtyards, entries, blank walls, poorly lit section of the school, inadequate signs, library stacks, or just plain eyesores.

Students could be asked to identify needs of these kinds throughout the school. Sometimes this may involve another content area and will require understanding the concepts and needs in that area. In exploring solutions, students might study color and other design applications in commercial displays, museum exhibits, and architectural super-graphics and placement of sculpture. Then, working if necessary with other departments in the school, students can change an area by mounting an exhibit, designing a bulletin board, producing sculpture, or redesigning the use of space.

Students who work in these areas learn that careers in this field involve working with the variable of human idiosyncrasies. The managerial function is necessary for these careers as well as the creative functions.

Unit Six	*Specific Careers*	*Related Careers*
	Sculptor	Technician
	Industrial designer	Management
	Aeronautical designer	Sales representative
	Automotive designer	Jewelry artisan
	Jewelry designer	Pottery artist
	Furniture designer	
	Potter	

The study of form and sculpture in a studio course offers many options for careers, and the practical aspects of a studio course offer many avenues of career exploration. Students begin by observing sculpture and three-dimensional design. Awareness of the sculptor's unique problems occurs as students move into designing their own projects. Study concerning well-known sculptors and the way they work leads to further consideration of techniques and esthetics. Carrying out a full-scale sculpture project enables students to play the role of a sculptor.

As they work, other careers may become apparent. For example, a sculptor may use a forge or work with neon light. Each technique involves skills and careers in some other field. Students may also learn that while the sculptor's function is primarily that of a creator, he or she may work with modules and become a re-creator as well. A sculptor often may need technical support to produce a sculpture, and if so, this will help students identify these related functions. In addition, the sculptor's efforts to sell the work are administrative or managerial tasks. Knowing more about this aspect may be helpful to students who are planning careers as agents or as sales representatives.

Students who are planning careers in construction or its related fields may find that many construction skills are similar to those used in sculpture. They may also find that the role of sculptor offers a satisfying means of personal expression.

Unit Seven

Specific Careers	*Related Careers*
Museum director	Researcher
Gallery owner	Writer
Curator	Critic
Docent/guide	Interpreter
Exhibit designer	Writer
Critic	
Art historian	
Education program specialist	

The function of critic and manager is vital to the majority of careers in this area. Students can lean about many of these art careers through field trips to museums, galleries, and art centers that are offered in the program. Often students may observe jobs that have never appeared within their range of possibilities.

To get the greatest benefit from these trips, students should visit behind the scenes in addition to taking a tour of the collection. There should be some discussion with professional personnel such as the museum director, curator, gallery owner, or docent. Other career opportunities that should be investigated by the students are the direction of special activities such as a children's program. Students who want to use verbal skills and foreign language skills may be interested in research jobs at an art institution, or in the production of educational materials for a museum or gallery. Also, the fact that many of these art centers offer careers in criticism and art history should be made evident to students.

Following a visit, students should identify the numerous jobs involved in a museum or gallery. One exercise might be to list the jobs. There might also be discussion of the career functions that were turned up in interviews with museum and art center personnel, supplemented by tapes and films about galleries and museums, and by study of art criticism and art history. Students interested in writing and history might obtain bibliographies from the publications department of a large gallery to guide them in their study of writing about art. Some students might benefit from working, possibly as volunteers, in a good museum or gallery program.

Specific Classroom Models

The suggested models below are not panaceas for all career education in the art classroom. There are hundreds of ways that art and art-related careers can be explored. The creative teacher can think of many other approaches to help students discover a future for themselves, occupationally or recreationally, in the field of art.

The basic aim of each model is to help students develop broad skills, knowledge, and understanding that are required for success in a variety of occupations rather than in a specific vocation. Even though there is some sense of chronology in the activities listed under the aims of each model, a specific activity might start at any level of the career development continuum.

Model A — *Commercial art and the world of work*

One aim of this course is to develop an awareness of the world of work through commercial art by:

1) Discussing with students the distinctions between film art and commercial art

2) Explaining the value of commercial art in the world of work

A second aim is to develop appreciation, knowledge, and understanding of the world of work through commercial art by:

1) Discussing with students the functions of an artist which relate to commercial art careers:

   a) The acts of creating — graphic designer, illustrator, display technician

   b) The acts of re-creating — production potter, production jeweler, production craftworker, other

   c) The acts of managing — art director, production coordinator, art supervisor, other

   d) Technical support — printer, draftsman or draftswoman, photographer, other

   e) Consumer criticism — art director, buyer, other

2) Discussing with students specific commercial art careers (in many cases, these careers are not mutually exclusive):

Fashion designer	Industrial designer
General illustrator	Display technician
Interior designer	Package designer
Magazine illustrator	Photographer
Advertising artist	Cartographer
Cartoonist	Toymaker
Editorial artist	Sign painter
Manuscript artist	Other
Medical illustrator	

3) Having students bring to class, identify, and discuss some commercial art commodities and relate them to the artists who created them:

Newspaper advertisements	Clothing
Magazine advertisements	Book illustrations
Films	Other
Package designs	

A third aim is to explore some of the career options in commercial art by:

1) Discussing with students what information and skills individuals need to make wise choices in considering commercial art careers

2) Reviewing the functions of the artist as they relate to commercial art

3) Having an art director from a local agency visit the classroom and talk to students about the operation and management of a commercial art agency or department and about careers in an agency

4) Making available to students promotional materials — pamphlets, brochures, films, and filmstrips — that have been obtained from agencies which produce them in their recruitment programs

5) Having staff artists visit the classroom to show and discuss commercial art models

6) Conducting a field trip to a commercial art agency, to an art department on a local newspaper or magazine, or to an art section of a government agency, and allowing students to observe and talk to artists to get behind-the-scenes views of the work

A fourth aim is to develop a simulated commercial art agency or department within the art classroom by:

1) Having students appoint a director and assistants in the class-room-designed agency (number of directors or assistants largely will be dependent upon how many different kinds of commercial art jobs the classroom agency will sponsor)

2) Presenting a demonstration of art materials and media used to produce commercial art objects

3) Having each director select his or her staff artists and decide on the items they will produce (director will make certain that each staff member follows the proper procedure for creating his or her art product)

4) Letting students develop fashion designs, brochures, book jackets, newspaper advertisements, and the like

5) Installing an exhibition in the school art gallery or at some other exhibition site of commercial art products created in the classroom simulation of an art agency

6) Conducting, with students, an evaluation of the art work and the entire experience

7) Finally, having students review and discuss points to consider when applying for a job or preparing for post-high school education (may take the form of a social drama, round-table discussion, or role playing; points to consider: personal appearance, command of subject matter, adequacy of skills, the application form procedure, the art portfolio, and financial matters)

A fifth aim is to have students participate in a few "hands-on" experiences in commercial art by:

1) Making personal contacts with commercial art firms or those with related jobs in the community

2) Finding out what jobs are available to students on a part-time basis

3) Planning a program with a distributive education teacher or a work-study coordinator in your school

4) Encouraging students interested in on-the-job experiences to serve as helpers and apprentices in private or government art departments

5) Having students interested in on-the-job experiences to serve as summer workers or interns as paste-up artists, sign painters, silk-screen apprentices, and the like

Model B — *Careers in visual arts via cooperative museum and school program*

This model should be taught in an art history, painting, drawing, or sculpture class. Precautions must be taken that art for its own sake not be disregarded and art which is merely a tool to explore careers be emphasized. Students should be involved in expressing their ideas and emotions through the art media, not in just studying careers. However, this type of unit would give them a realistic view of what the artist does in performing as an artist.

The first aim of this model is to make students aware of the role of the artist in the world of work by:

1) Discussing with students the role of the artist in society as a painter or sculptor who seeks only self-fulfillment through his or her medium

2) Discussing the role of the artist in society as a painter or sculptor who creates works of art as a service for others

3) Having an artist discuss with students his or her attitudes toward work and responsibilities to self, home, and society

A second aim is to make students aware of careers in the visual arts through a study of five functions of the artist by performing the activities below. None of these functions is mutually exclusive, for artists may perform one or more while working at their profession.

1) Having students list as many occupations as they can of artists involved in the following careers:

a) Careers in creating

Painter	Architect
Sculptor	City planner
Ceramist	Fashion designer
Set designer	Industrial designer
Interior decorator	Other
Display technician	

b) Careers in re-creating

Production potter	Production craftworker
Production jeweler	Conservationist
Production printmaker	Other
Foundry worker	

c) Careers in management

Art director	Small art gallery owner
Art teacher	Antique dealer
Curator	Gift and art shop owner
Production coordinator	Other

d) Careers in technical support

Printer	Photographer
Foundry worker	Draftsman or
Museum technologist	draftswoman
Gallery staff	Other

e) Careers in criticism on behalf of the consumer

Art director	Fashion coordinator
Art critic	Art teacher
Art historian	Other

2) Having students discuss these occupations and how they pertain to an artist

A third aim in this model is to have students create objects of art for their own self-satisfaction, and to get a feel of what the artist experiences when he or she is creating, by performing the activities listed below. These activities can be shared by teachers of other subject matter in an interdisciplinary humanities program, thus showing students in a dramatic way how art relates to all disciplines and offers a broad range of career options.

1) Having students express, through painting, their ideas and emotions concerning humankind and nature, such as:

a) Pondering the mysteriousness of nature

b) Celebrating the beauties of nature

c) Glorifying nature

d) In conflict with nature

e) Being concerned about the perils of the environment

f) Considering one's relationship to nature

g) Searching nature for the ultimate truth

h) Considering one's relationship to animals

i) Deliberating the old saw, "man's inhumanity to man"

j) Searching oneself for an identity

k) Celebrating the achievements of humankind

2) Having students view and study some of the works of the masters in art and sculpture that are centered round the above ideas

3) Contemplating the works of the following great artists:

Bosch	Giotto	Raphael
Boucher	Goya	Rembrandt
Brueghel	Greco, El	Renoir
Cézanne	Hogarth	Rubens
Cimabue	Holbein	Titian
Constable	Ingres	Turner
Dali	Laurens	Vasari
David	Manet	Velásquez
da Vinci	Masaccio	Vermeer
Degas	Michelangelo	Whistler
Dürer	Millet	Wood
Gauguin	Picasso	Wyeth

A fourth aim in this model is to have students, through museum field trips and discussions with art specialists, study careers in an art museum by:

1) Having students explore careers involved in a work of art from its creation to its acquisition by a museum ("occupational lineage" of a work of art)

a) Artist creating the work of art

b) Critic analyzing the work of art

c) Historian analyzing, evaluating, and interpreting the work of art

d) Museum director purchasing the work of art

e) Curator storing the work of art

f) Exhibit specialist displaying the work of art

g) Cataloguer recording the work of art for publication

h) Docent explaining the work of art to the public

i) Education specialist designing programs for students round the work of art

j) Teacher using the work of art as an original resource for classroom activities

k) Conservationist keeping the work of art in the proper environment and keeping it clean

l) Guard protecting the work of art from damage and theft

m) Gallery staff packing and shipping the work of art for other exhibits

2) Having artists, critics, historians, and curators visit the classroom to discuss their specialist roles, preferably before the class makes a museum visit

3) Having specialists, when possible, demonstrate their specialties

4) Providing opportunities in which students can observe specialists at work in their studios and museums

A fifth aim is to provide students with on-the-job experiences in museums and other agencies by:

1) Making personal contacts with museums and other agencies in order to help students get jobs

2) Finding out what jobs are available to students on a part-time basis

3) Planning a program with a distributive education teacher or a work-study coordinator in your school

4) Encouraging students interested in on-the-job experience to serve as apprentices, docents, student researchers, framers, exhibit helpers, and the like

5) Encouraging students to participate in specially designed educational programs:

a) Career day

b) Portfolio day

c) Summer internships

d) Museum media workshops

e) Museum training programs

f) Museum volunteer programs

g) Student art research

Model C — *Establishing an art resource center in the school*

An art resource center can provide many useful materials and facilities for student consideration of art and art-related careers. Print and nonprint media pertaining to careers in art should be listed in this center, as they have proved to be valuable in this field. The materials should be available for use by students, parents, counselors, community resource people, and other teaching staff for the exploration of a variety of careers.

Exemplary models for career education programs in art can provide certain strategies through which to approach the problem. Ultimately, the teacher must develop his or her own programs to deal with specific situations.

Conclusion

It is clear today that art careers, art-related careers, and careers which are made more meaningful by acquaintance with art processes must be a significant focus of the art educator. Painting, sculpture, and other art activities, while vital and important in themselves, can be made far more meaningful to students if the art educator is sensitive to the needs all students will have when they enter the working world beyond the classroom.

Selected References

American Art Directory. For the American Federation of Arts. New York: R. R. Bowker Company.

Biegeleisen, J. I. *Careers and Opportunities in Commercial Art.* New York: E. P. Dutton & Co., Inc. 1963.

Coyne, John; and Herbert, Tom. *By Hand: A Guide to Schools and Careers in Crafts.* New York: E. P. Dutton & Co., Inc.

DeLong, Fred. *Aim for a Job in Drafting.* New York: Richards Rosen Press, Inc. 1967.

"Fashion Designing." College and career article no. 296. *Mademoiselle.*

"Fashion Design Schools." College and career article no. 3389. *Mademoiselle.*

Frazier, John; and Julin, Richard. *Your Future in Landscape Architecture.* New York: Richards Rosen Press, Inc. 1967.

Fried, Eleanor L. *Is the Fashion Business Your Business?* New York: Fairchild Publications, Inc. 1961.

Fujita, Neil. *Aim for a Job in Graphic Art/Design.* New York: Richards Rosen Press, Inc. 1969.

Greer, Michael. *Your Future in Interior Design.* New York: Richards Rosen Press, Inc.

Head, Edith. *Fashion as a Career.* New York: Julian Messner, Publishers, Inc. 1966.

Johnson, George. *Your Career in Advertising.* New York: Julian Messner, Publishers, Inc. 1966.

Keppler, Victor. *Your Future in Photography.* New York: Richards Rosen Press, Inc. 1973.

Margolius, Sidney. *Planning for College: A Complete Guide to Selection, Admission, Financing.* New York: Avon Books Division, The Hearst Corporation. 1965.

McLaughlin, Robert W. *Architect: Creating Man's Environment.* New York: The Macmillan Company. 1962.

Minnesota Department of Employment Security. "Draftsman: An Occupational Guide." St. Paul: Minnesota Department of Employment Security. 1960.

Musial, Joseph W. "Comic Art." Manhassett, Long Island, New York: Joseph W. Musial. 1962.

National Art Education Association. *American Artist Art School Directory.* Reston, Virginia: National Art Education Association.

_____. "Teaching Art as a Career." Reston Virginia: National Art Education Association.

Neblette, C. B. "Careers in Photography." Rochester, New York: Rochester Institute of Technology. 1965.

Nelson, Roy Paul; and Ferris, Byron. *Fell's Guide to Commercial Art.* New York: Frederick Fell, Inc. 1966.

Philadelphia College of Art, Office of Public Information. "Your Career in Art." Philadelphia: Philadelphia College of Fine Art. 1967.

Rodewald, Fred C.; and Gotschall, Edward M. *Commercial Art as a Business.* New York: The Viking Press, Inc. 1960.

Roth, Richard. *Your Future in Architecture.* New York: Richards Rosen Press, Inc. 1969.

Science Research Associates, Inc. *Jobs in Art.* Chicago: Science Research Associates, Inc. 1966.

U.S. Department of Health, Education, and Welfare, Office of Education. *A Guide to Student Assistance.* Washington, D.C.: U.S. Government Printing Office. 1970.

"Working in Crafts." College and career article no. 324. *Mademoiselle.*

Your Future in Fashion Design. New York: Richards Rosen Press, Inc. 1969.

7
Revitalizing Foreign Language Instruction through Career Education

American Council on the Teaching of Foreign Languages

C. Edward Scebold
Executive Secretary

Richard Brod
Association of Departments of Foreign Languages
New York, New York

Dora Kennedy
Prince George's County Public Schools
Upper Marlboro, Maryland

Joanna Crane
Alabama State Department of Education
Montgomery Alabama

Ms. Toby Tamarkin
Manchester Community College
Manchester, Connecticut

7
Career Education in the Foreign Language Classroom

"Language," Thomas Mann said, "is civilization itself." But in recent years, the public school teaching of foreign languages — modern as well as ancient — has been subject to declining enrollments accompanied by charges of irrelevance. In a preliminary report on a survey of 1974 fall enrollments, the Modern Language Association says that since 1965 the proportion of colleges that require entering students to have studied a foreign language dropped from 33.6 to 19.4 percent. Only 56 percent of the colleges were making the study of a foreign language a prerequisite for the bachelor's degree — down from 88.9 percent.

Why should foreign languages continue to be taught when students and colleges alike apparently see less need for them? An old argument, used with secondary school students who raised questions about the relevance of foreign language study to their lives, was that these languages are an indispensable component of college preparation. Obviously, this argument no longer has much validity. It is clear that foreign language instruction — like many things that have long been accepted — must readdress itself to modern needs. At the same time, it must maintain its integrity as a discipline with vital functions: to carry forward, from the human past, rich resources of knowledge, understanding, and experience, and to serve as a unifying force among peoples and nations.

It is the public school sector of foreign language instruction that is in trouble. Enrollments are booming in private language schools. Moreover, the sites in which the study of languages takes place have spread in recent years throughout the community. It is not uncommon for classes to meet in church basements, neighborhood centers, private homes, places of business, and manpower training centers.

The need for language study in human resource training for disadvantaged persons highlights some of the practical considerations that those who teach foreign languages should take into account. In the mid-1960s, when the federal government began to focus on the employment situation of the disadvantaged — their lack of skills and of jobs — skills training programs were set up in an attempt to remedy the problem. However, many disadvantaged persons could not benefit from these programs because their capabilities in any language, including their own, were so seriously deficient that they could not deal with textbook material or with later demands that would be made of them in a job. One response to these needs was to set up English as a second language (ESL) training courses, which have proved to be remarkably successful in building language competencies in a relatively short time among persons with little previous education or language skills. It is noteworthy that these courses have been largely oriented toward helping students meet a practical goal: getting a job in which they can make a living.

The questions remain whether public schools can meet today's foreign language needs and whether the schools can help students find viable relationships between foreign language study and what it takes to function ably as an adult. Some giant steps have already been taken toward providing answers to these questions. During the past fifteen years, foreign language teaching in public schools has undergone a revolution of sorts. The earlier emphasis on teaching students to read and write other languages has given way to an emphasis on oral and aural skills — speaking and understanding a language with the purpose of achieving first those communications skills that are most useful in everyday life. As students progress in the study of a language, they build up their reading and writing skills, enabling them to explore in greater depth other models of thought and value systems and to learn more about the roots and linkages of languages.

Career education and foreign language instruction have many significant mutual interests. While career education is concerned with the total development of students in their preparation for adult working life, in the foreign language sector, it provides a way for students to relate their foreign language learning to their growing awareness of their own career goals and potential — and all without altering the traditional values of the discipline. Identification of learning goals with career goals can strengthen motivation and achievement while encouraging students to select and evaluate their curriculum on a rational basis. Career education also gives language educators an opportunity to reach a broader segment of the student population than they have attracted in years past.

In most schools, foreign language instruction is elective and not generally available until the seventh or even the ninth grade. By then, many students have been conditioned to make career choices — sometimes extremely narrow ones — that relate to their perceptions of themselves and their perceptions of what teachers and other people think of them. Because language study has often been justified as an indispensable component of college preparation and its educational goals (both its linguistic skills and its humanistic content) have been seen in this context, the tendency has been to discourage large numbers of students.

So far as linguistic skills are concerned, most students — even those who have never studied a foreign language — can readily come to understand the relevance of these skills to real and potential careers. A substantial body of data has been compiled to demonstrate the value of supportive language skills in a wide variety of occupations. The humanistic values of language study are less obvious, and educators will need to seek ways to present and explicate these values to their current and potential students by providing a new rationale for language study in terms of students' career goals and developmental choices.

Career education is not synonymous with the dispensing of occupational information. It is not intended to conflict with other important educational objectives. Its proponents point out that the beneficiaries of career education can still become good citizens, parents, and cultivated and self-aware human beings because career success can augment all other sound educational objectives. These proponents recognize that an academic discipline implies a basic core of knowledge, skills, and attitudes which are to be learned if one is to be conversant with that discipline. The thrust of career education is to reinforce this basic core in all disciplines. Dr. Kenneth Hoyt, who has written extensively about career education, states that "to build a career education learning experience without paying careful attention to the academic skills to be mastered during the project is to defeat one of the most important reasons for the whole career education movement."

This position makes it clear that the aims of career education are not at cross-purposes with the humanistic aims of foreign language study. Actually, the two parallel processes converge in shaping self-fulfilled individuals — people who understand the relationships between education and career opportunities, and who are interested in their own and other cultures and in all of the many heritages that make up the humanities.

Indeed the study of foreign languages persists as a basic tool for helping students expand their sensitivity to human beings round the world, and to understand both the bonds that unite and the differences that separate them. Through language study, students can acquire: (1) an increased awareness of language as a mode of communication and as a system for organizing thought, (2) a heightened sensitivity to linguistic and cultural differences both within the United States and globally, (3) an understanding of the principle that cultures can be compared and contrasted with one another without being ranked, (4) a recognition of the increasing internationalization of all aspects of contemporary life — social, economic, political, scientific, and artistic, (5) an understanding and appreciation of a specific target culture, and (6) varying degrees of competence in the skills of listening, speaking, reading, and writing a second language. Essentially, the result is that the study of foreign languages helps students define and pursue their own life values, whether vocational or avocational, or both.

The goals of career education are to provide students with opportunities for exploration, familiarization, preparation, and selection of a meaningful work role. These goals are concerned with career development, skills development, motivation for learning, and the development of an understanding of the world of work and an appreciation of the individual's place in that world. In reaching these goals, career education is not another study unit to be covered by a teacher during the school year. Rather, career education calls for a refocusing of daily course content so that there is maintained a high degree of relevance and student motivation in what the teacher presents.

Every academic discipline has career implications in its substantive content for some students. The sequential stages of career education are awareness, exploration, decision making, and preparation. Most of the goals inherent in these stages are compatible with the substantive content of foreign language learning. For example, the goals for the awareness stage include an understanding of the life-styles, values, major duties, and responsibilities involved in a broad range of career areas, and the relationship of the acquisition of basic communications skills to many future roles. If foreign language study begins in elementary grades, the usual time for awareness to appear in the career development spectrum is at this level. However, many schools do not offer foreign language study until the high school years. Then awareness must start with the foreign language experience at that level.

Students are likely to enter their first foreign language class with some experience in exploring career options. This experience can be expanded and enhanced by the systematic examination of the relationship of foreign language skills as tools or as background in a wide variety of careers. It should soon become apparent to them that foreign language study is related both developmentally and attitudinally to the career education process. Indeed both career education and foreign language learning are process oriented. In the process of learning a foreign language, students can be exposed to work concepts and work values as they exist both in the target culture and, by comparison, in their own culture.

As students progress in the foreign language sequence, they should become more sophisticated about their knowledge of specific language skills vis-à-vis careers as they develop fluency and become better able to discuss these matters in the target language. Some of these students may choose to emphasize one or two foreign language skills rather than all four (listening, speaking, reading, and writing). The relationship of foreign language competency to careers may be viewed as a continuum, spanning the need for foreign languages as a primary skill, as a coequal skill, as an adjunct skill, or as valuable background. Students should be made aware of this continuum through direct teaching and through activities that enable them to discover these relationships.

The goals of the investigative and decision-making stages of career education include a greater knowledge of self, plus the in-depth study of a number of career possibilities which relates these possibilities to the individual's developing talents and interests. Another dimension is added to possible career choices by their examining the world of work as represented in the fifteen occupational clusters that have been identified by the U.S. Office of Education. These clusters and possible foreign language-related occupations are as follows:

(1) Agri-business and natural resources

Translator of technical writing	Interpreter for export and import firms
Secretary	Geologist
Peace Corps member	

(2) Business and office

Foreign exchange clerk	Market specialist
Credit manager	Lawyer
Receptionist	Stenographer
Sales representative	Teller
Certified public accountant	

(3) Communications and media

Actor	Correspondent
Telephone operator	Telegrapher

(4) Consumer and homemaking education

Dietician	Consumer expert
Fashion buyer	Tailor
Chef	Wine expert

(5) Construction

Architect	Engineer
Supervisor	Planner
Translator	Secretarial worker

(6) Environmental control

Translator	Technical writer
Researcher	Interpreter

(7) Fine arts and humanities

Artist	Actor
Curator	Archeologist
Cryptographer	Librarian
Drama coach	Teacher
Composer	Author
Singer	

(8) Health

Medical librarian	X-ray technician
Medical secretary	Physician
Lab technician	Interpreter
Dentist	Nurse
Nurse's aide	Hospital orderly

(9) Hospitality and recreation

Travel guide	Opera singer
Hotel worker	Drama coach
Tour conductor	Critic
Clerk	Travel agency secretary

(10) Manufacturing

Buyer	Manager
Inspector	Supervisor
Technical writer	Branch manager

(11) Marine science

Merchant marine	Marine biologist
Radio operator	Oceanographer

(12) Marketing and distribution

Buyer	Clerk
Sales representative	Secretary
Advertising specialist	Translator for import and export firms
Writer	Printer

(13) Personal services

Usher	Barber
Butler	Beautician
Missionary	Postal clerk
Cosmetologist	Travel companion
Interpreter	Translator
Receptionist	Secretary

(14) Public services

Missionary	FBI agent
Foreign news interpreter	Immigration inspector
Firefighter	Diplomat
Lawyer	

(15) Transportation

Guide	Flight attendant
Purser	Travel agent
Stewardess	Steward
Ticket agent	Pilot

These are but a few of the occupations found within these fifteen clusters; students will be able to come up with many more during their career exploration of how career education pertains to foreign languages. Students should also investigate the world of work in the target culture, not only in the central locations of that culture but also in other geographical locations, including ethnic communities in the United States.

The goals in the exploration and decision-making stages of career education are expanded considerably by the almost limitless opportunities that the study of a modern or classical language opens up, because it shapes a usable tool and a background for many jobs in business, health occupations, communications and media, social service occupations, voluntarism, and the like. Although career education is concerned with the development of the total person within the work context, students also should recognize the complementary functions that knowing a foreign language and culture can serve in avocational pursuits such as travel, reading, and appreciation of the arts and humanities.

The goals of the preparation stage of career education in foreign languages can be implemented only partially in the senior high school. However, possibilities for this should not be overlooked. In addition to the sequential program, in which foreign languages and career development are related as an ongoing process, a number of vocationally oriented mini-courses can be set up to meet student needs and interests. A few quality courses of this type are recommended rather than a proliferation of such courses. These mini-courses can also be incorporated into advanced levels of the sequential program, but they need not — and probably should not — constitute the entire upper level program. What these mini-courses can add to the curriculum is a feature which makes it possible for students who are not planning to continue their formal education after high school to use foreign language skills in entry-level jobs.

Relating Teaching to Career Education

How can the teacher who recognizes the importance of career education in foreign language implement this idea? First of all, the teacher must be motivated to find ways to relate what is going on in his or her classroom, and on the outside, with the world of work — that segment of the world in which a conscious effort is made to produce goods and services for the benefit of oneself and of others. The teacher's motivation may be a natural outcropping of the teacher's own explorations in the world of work, whether through research, in-service study, or employment in a nonteaching position during the summer months or other noncontract period. Once the classroom teacher's own horizons have been broadened, resulting in a desire to implement the comprehensive career education concept, the task of motivating students becomes easier.

The role of the classroom teacher in the correlation of foreign language study and its career implications consists of the following:

(1) To devise and locate methods and materials designed to help students understand and appreciate the career implications of foreign language study

(2) To use career-oriented methods and materials in the program, where appropriate, as a means to gain educational motivation

(3) To identify occupations and match skills

(4) To relate regular classroom experiences and materials to the career education activities in foreign language studies

(5) To help students acquire and use good work habits

(6) To help students acquire decision-making skills

(7) To help students develop, clarify, and assimilate personally meaningful sets of work values

(8) To integrate, as fully as possible, the programmatic assumption of career education into language activities and teacher-student relationships

(9) To highlight the world of work in the target culture as well as within different ethnic groups in the United States

(10) To provide students, if necessary, with specific vocational competencies at a level that will enable them to get jobs

(11) To help students, if necessary, acquire job seeking and job acquisition skills

(12) To participate at times in the job placement process

Teaching Strategies

There are a number of ways to relate different stages of career education to foreign language studies. One of the most useful is to correlate regular textbook materials and classroom techniques with career development concepts. First, teachers and students should be aware of the potential and the limitations in careers for which knowledge of a second language is a primary skill — chiefly teaching, translating, and oral interpreting. In general, the job requirements for translating and interpreting careers are stringent; they are more demanding than teaching; and positions in these fields are relatively few. These occupations should not generally be recommended to an average student of languages. Moreover, at present it is unrealistic and misleading for teachers to suggest that there are readily available translating or interpreting jobs available in the U.S. government or in the United Nations.

What teachers should emphasize in discussing career uses of language skills is the wide variety of positions for which knowledge of a foreign language is an important ancillary or supportive skill. The range of positions is so considerable that these occupations can be found in any one of the fifteen U.S. Office of Education career clusters. There is a useful listing of such careers, accompanied by illustrations, anecdotes, and statistics, in the pamphlet, "Foreign Languages and Careers," published by the Modern Language Association. The list of positions extends from the entry level to executive or professional status, and it covers such diverse fields as business and industry (sales, engineering, banking, secretarial); civil service (foreign service, Peace Corps, education, law, library science);

media (radio, television, film, newspapers, and other types of publishing); science, health services (doctors, nurses, nurses' aides, health advocates); academic social sciences; and travel and tourism. Examples of jobs range from taxi driver or hotel receptionist to foreign correspondents and executives in multinational corporations. In each case, language skills enhance and extend the job seeker's specialized preparation and enable him or her to apply for a wider range of positions. The job options may include posts with U.S. firms overseas, with branches of foreign firms located in the U.S., and with urban community groups that serve non-English–speaking peoples.

Teachers should make students aware that acquiring second language skills will broaden their options in any of the career areas mentioned and in many cases will increase their earning capacity as well. A recent survey made by the Modern Language Association found that more than 70 percent of U.S. business firms report that second language skills are important in some way in their business operations. Some were actively seeking employees with functional language skills and sensitivity to social and cultural differences among peoples. Worldwide, English is the accepted language of the business world. When U.S. firms send specialists out of the country, they select those who go on the basis of their expertise in a specialty, such as sales or engineering, rather than for their language skills. However, a survey being made for the U.S. Office of Education is finding that businesses would prefer the people they send to be able to function well in the language of the host country. Many firms express the view that when the sole reliance is on English in business dealings, serious human relations barriers exist which can be extremely difficult to overcome.

Starting at the awareness stage of career education development, the teacher should not only enhance students' knowledge of career choices in which foreign languages are useful, but should also help students develop self-awareness of their own interests and potential in terms of such careers. There are many classroom activities to help develop both self-awareness and knowledge of careers in which foreign language is an additional tool. The following models are presented as examples of career education exercises that can be done in the foreign language classroom.

Model A — *Career awareness*

A two-stage exercise can help students examine their own interests and strong points and then relate what they learn to career choices.

1) Have the students list five things they have done in school (be it elementary, junior high, or high school) or in their free time of which they are proud. Next, have them list five things that they think they do well. Notice that these are *positive* items to help students feel good about themselves and begin looking at their own capabilities. When the list has been completed, have the students go over it once more to number the five items according to the following:

   a)   Place a "1" after any item that required working with other people.

   b)   Place a "2" after any item that required working alone.

   c)   Place a "3" after any item that was more dependent upon physical effort.

   d)   Place a "4" after any item that was more dependent upon mental effort.

   e)   Place a "5" after any item in which the student was a leader.

   f)   Place a "6" after any item in which achievement involved some sort of competition.

After the students have completed (a) through (f) above, have them discuss what they have discovered (or simply tell the class about the item that scored most often on their list).

2) Have the students list five jobs that they might consider as their adult "career." After completing the list, the students should answer questions such as:

   a)   Does anyone in my family work in this career?

   b)   Do I know anyone in this career?

   c)   Have I done any reading about this career?

   d)   Have I spoken to anyone about what the career is like?

   e)   What is the approximate salary for this career choice?

   f)   Does the career require more use of head or of hands?

   g)   Is there special training required?

   h)   Is college necessary?

   i)   Is this position available near my home?

   j)   Will I work more with people or with things?

k) Will the work be done indoors or out-of-doors?

l) Will the work schedule be fixed or flexible?

m) Will I have a supervisor or will I be relatively independent in my work?

n) Will I wear a uniform?

o) Is travel involved?

The student will then discuss their possible career choices and the reasons for their preferences. Another follow-up activity would be a discussion of what the students learned about themselves and their interests. They might complete the statement, "I was surprised to learn..." or "I discovered that...." Depending upon the level of the language course, these exercises will be either in English or in the target language.

After the students have completed all of the above, the teacher will go round the room and check *one* of the five career selections each student has made. The career should be one in which foreign language is a major prerequisite or an adjunct tool. The teacher will then write the title of that career in the foreign language for each student. Students will then prepare at home, in the library, or in class (using resource materials) a brief job description in the target language. The description might include:

1) Place of work (institution)

2) Work hours

3) Probable salary

4) Major responsibilities

5) Skills needed other than foreign language

These short descriptions may be presented orally to the class, and the teacher can question the class about the information presented. The descriptions also may be written out with a picture of the job attached, if possible, and placed on a bulletin board or displayed in some other manner. Good resources that help students learn about careers in the target culture are foreign language newspapers, magazines, and foreign editions of telephone directories (yellow pages). The directories are available in public libraries or may be purchased from the local telephone company.

The teacher can prepare a dialogue presentation which includes several occupations. The class can discuss these occupations and decide whether the careers are closely associated with the target culture or are universal occupations.

When concentrating on a specific unit, such as transportation, sports, tourism, communications systems, buying or selling, and the like, the teacher should build in activities that relate to the world of work. Through field trips, class visits by workers, student projects, or role playing, the vocabulary units can also become career units.

Model B — *Career exploration*

In orientation and exploration, the second stage of career education development, each student should get a more comprehensive treatment of the careers that involve knowledge of a second language and that have been selected as interesting by the students and the teacher. The following sample exercises encompass the career exploration component of career education.

Sample Exercise 1 — Exploring careers in foreign language

In this exercise, the teacher will guide the students in the following:

a) Bring in a resource person who can be interviewed by the class and who will answer many specific questions about a particular career choice.

b) Show a film or a filmstrip that relates foreign languages to different types of careers.

c) Visit a business or other organization in the community where second language proficiency is required or useful.

d) Have students choose different occupational clusters and investigate occupations within the clusters that can be related to foreign language skills. (The students might prepare charts with this information and discuss these in class. The charts can continue to be useful if posted in classrooms or near the school's guidance offices.)

Sample Exercise 2 — Holding a foreign language career orientation fair

Invite from ten to twenty people in the community to spend a morning at your school. These guests will meet with students in small groups to discuss informally their own occupations for about half an hour. To give students a chance to explore at least three careers, three consecutive sessions might be held. Afterwards, students and guests could have a social period with refreshments and opportunity for further career discussions.

Sample Exercise 3 — "Listen and guess"

The teacher might prepare an audio cassette that lists job descriptions in the target language. Help in preparation of the cassette might be obtained from other language teachers and from native speakers in the community. After the cassette is viewed, students are asked to guess each profession that has been described. Flash cards picturing various professions and giving job titles in a foreign language are available from commercial firms in French, Spanish, and German.

Sample Exercise 4 — Role simulation mini-courses

Ten-week courses dealing with a specific career area in terms of its foreign language needs can be prepared so that students can move from career exploration to role simulation. This will help them decide if a specific job is suitable for them. Such a program was prepared by Patricia Breiner of Cincinnati, Ohio, on travel and trade careers. A group of careers in this category was studied in depth, with students watching actual job procedures on field trips and filling out various job forms for practice purposes. Students also simulated some of the career roles. For example, they conducted tours in the target language for other language students and called attention to points of interest in the high school complex. Most of the materials used to prepare this mini-course were obtained from government agencies. These materials dealt with immigration, passports, currency, rate of exchange, and the like. Similar mini-courses in German are successfully being used at Ridgefield High School in Connecticut.

Sample Exercise 5 — Students teaching students

Another idea is to have advanced foreign language students put together and run a mini-course for students in other courses. For example, they might teach some functional vocabulary and language skills to students in vocational education courses such as food services, cosmetology, and auto mechanics. This type of program is being used by Barbara Bigelow at Crossland High School in Prince George's County, Maryland.

Sample Exercise 6 — Surveying for present and future needs

As students get ready to narrow down career opportunities to specific jobs they find desirable, they must determine the current level of demand for workers in these occupations and the entry-level job requirements. They should ask themselves whether they will need to get some post-secondary education; whether their use of a foreign language in the occupation will be a primary, ancillary, or adjunct skill; and whether they will need to take more foreign language study.

Crossland Senior High School has also tried activities in some of these areas. Foreign language students have surveyed local businesses to find out present and future needs for workers with a second language. This survey information is useful to the entire school because, in addition to turning up information on foreign language needs, the survey provides a profile of business opportunities in the area.

A typical survey, printed here to stimulate the teacher's and students' imagination, is as follows:

a) Type of business _____

b) Number of employees _____

c) Location (local, state, or regional) _____

d) Do any of your customers or clients use or speak a foreign language? (Leave room for "yes" and "no" boxes.)

e) Do you presently employ people with foreign language skills? ("Yes and "no" boxes.)

f) Are applicants with foreign language skills preferable? ("Yes" and "no" boxes.)

g) What percentage of your employees have at least one foreign language skill?

_____ less than 25% _____ 26 to 50% _____ more than 50%

h) Please check the foreign language skills that you would consider most important for employees of the following categories:

	Listening	Speaking	Reading	Writing
Clerical-secretarial				
Sales				
Technical				
Managerial				
Executive				

i) In which of these employment areas do you expect a need to arise (or increase) in the next two to three years. Please check.

	Expect need to arise	Expect need to increase	Estimated number of new positions
Clerical-secretarial			
Sales			
Technical			
Managerial			
Executive			

j) Please check the languages which would be beneficial to employees in your business setting. If more than one language, please number in the order of their importance (1 = most important, and so forth).

_____ Spanish   _____ Russian   Others (please specify)

_____ French   _____ Japanese   _____

_____ German   _____ Korean   _____

k) Would anyone in your company be available to speak at a local secondary school on the importance of foreign language skills in your business? ("Yes" and "no" boxes.)

l) Other comments: _____

_____

m) Position of person completing survey (optional):

_____

Sample Exercise 7 — Foreign language and the communications media

Still another exercise that can be integrated easily into the more advanced level of a foreign language career emphasis is the preparation of a biweekly or monthly newspaper by all language classes in the school. This can be done in cooperation with the journalism staff. The newspaper articles can be done either on a voluntary basis or as written class assignments, and they can recount current events in the school.

Another approach is to have foreign language students present, in the target language, once-a-week announcements of major events over the school's loudspeaker system. The language used for these announcements might change from week to week. These exercises are particularly useful to students interested in newspaper, radio, and public relations jobs.

Sample Exercise 8 — Careers for Spanish-speaking Americans

One example of the way that an industrious teacher can help students prepare for specific careers that require or benefit from some knowledge of a foreign language is the course in career Spanish prepared by Tony Tamarkin at Manchester Community College in Connecticut. Although this program is considered a second-year language course, it has many features which can be adapted by the secondary school teacher.

Realizing the need for a more practical approach to language learning in the Northeast, especially at the community college level, Ms. Tamarkin prepared materials for an audiovisual "Career Spanish" course. She wanted to draw from the community at large those workers whose jobs called for an understanding of Spanish as well as those students in the college enrolled in a specific program that would place them in contact with the Spanish-speaking community.

This course has three focal points: medical careers, public service careers, and business careers. There are 24 lessons in all, which consist of the following materials:

a) Three- to four-minute television dialogue (often filmed on location for better role simulation)

    b) Overhead transparency containing the written dialogue

    c) Three-page student lesson:

      1) Page 1, new vocabulary

      2) Page 2, grammatical review

      3) Page 3, additional questions related to job procedures

    d) Audio cassette:

      1) Part 1, pronunciation practice with the dialogue and vocabulary list

      2) Part 2, grammatical exercises using present, preterit, imperfect, and future tenses

      3) Part 3, an oral practice using the additional questions in the student lesson

    e) Mimeographed materials — welfare applications, charge account applications, hospital admissions questionnaires, and so forth

For example, lessons in the medical section include: emergency situation 1 (possible appendicitis), emergency situation 2 (nausea and fainting), hospital admissions (personal and medical history), pregnancy, taking a blood test, taking an X ray, occupational therapy, dental hygiene, and the visiting nurse.

After representatives of other colleges visited the program, it received full transfer credit in Connecticut. Any student or member of the community with two years of high school Spanish or a year of college Spanish may take the course, which is given in the evening to accommodate everyone. At the end of two semesters, students and workers in this program are able to understand and speak Spanish within their chosen professions. They do not merely utter commands, but can actively communicate and handle their entire occupational roles in the second language.

The results are directly related to the materials, which took three years to prepare. These materials completely immerse the student in the second language. They bombard the student's senses — sight, sound, and even touch as the student handles the different instruments necessary in an occupation — while simulating job procedures in the classroom.

The students begin with a televised dialogue. They recognize the type of job and the essence of what is happening because television uses a combination of sound and sight. The native speakers do not slow their speech, and all extraneous noises on the job have been retained on the television tape in order to keep the situation as close as possible to real life. The teacher reviews the specific vocabulary with the student, acting out and gesturing to show word meaning whenever possible, before the initial viewing of the televised dialogue.

The students know that only Spanish is spoken unless the teacher is discussing some cultural aspect or a very difficult point in the lesson.

After the first viewing of the filmed dialogue, the students see the script on an overhead transparency. The teacher asks simple questions of all the students, who use the dialogue as an aid. The teacher points to the answer so that the student is not at a loss for words. Then students watch the dialogue on television a second time. This time they understand a great deal more and again use the dialogue transparency, although the teacher now discusses each question or bit of information in a personalized manner. For example, "Did you ever take a blood test?" "Where did you take it?" "Were you comfortable in the office?" "Did you like it?" "Does it hurt?" "Why did you need the test?"

At its next meeting, the class helps the teacher prepare a synthesis of the job procedure which is shown on the overhead transparency. Below is an example of such a synthesis in "Taking a Blood Test." This particular lesson is done in Spanish, but it could be done in any other language as well. The English translation (in parentheses), which can be transformed into other languages, is provided.

a) Identificación: "Buenos días. Yo soy el técnico."

(Identification: "Good morning. I am the technician.")

b) Explicación de por qué el paciente está aquí.

(Explanation of why the patient is here.)

c) Explicación de la prueba de sangre: "No se ponga nervioso."

(Explanation of the blood test: "Don't be nervous.")

d) "¿Ha comido o bebido desde la medianoche?"

("Have you eaten or drunk [anything] since midnight?")

e) La prueba: "Suba la manga; la banda apretada; haga un puño; guarde el brazo derecho; es sólo un pequeño pinchazo; no le dolerá. No se mueva."

(The test: "Roll up your sleeve; [I am making] the band tight; make a fist; keep your arm straight; it's only a small prick; it will not hurt. Don't move.")

The synthesis is necessary to get the actual sequence of events in a particular job in focus in both the instructor's and the students' minds. The students work in groups of two or three, playing different roles until they have mastered the lesson. When they are ready, they tell the teacher and take an oral exam. Either the classroom teacher, another foreign language speaker, or student will play the opposite role (patient, client, customer). The burden of getting and giving all pertinent information rests with the students being tested.

The program has been so successful in reaching its major goal — to build student fluency in the chosen occupational situation — that these materials are being tried experimentally for persons in the community who have never studied Spanish, and they also will be used for an in-service course at Hartford Hospital.

Using this type of material as a first approach to learning Spanish necessitates a much slower pace with each dialogue than is usually the case, and this must be a specific lesson arrangement (beginning with the shortest, grammatically easiest lesson, and progressing to the more difficult unit). Although the beginning student cannot be expected to be fluent in the language, he or she should be able to master a great deal of needed vocabulary, basic verbs and pronouns, and adequate pronunciation.

During one semester the teacher allowed students to choose the lessons they wanted to learn. Of necessity, no more than three different units could be studied at one time in the classroom. This enabled the teacher to work with each of the three groups on the overhead transparency during the class period. The teacher did not allow this freedom of choice until students had worked together through the first two units and understood the methodology being used and the routines involved in learning each lesson. The technique is especially well suited to a classroom where a teacher's aide or student helper is available.

This is an exciting program, using all possible attention getters. The teacher is rewarded with appreciative students, happy times with a "fun" method, and concrete results in terms of job needs.

Sample Exercise 9 — Foreign language in aviation

A good example of how to gear career emphasis to local needs is a program at August Martin High School in Jamaica, New York, where many courses have emphasis on aviation. The school, located one mile from Kennedy International Airport, is a comprehensive high school that offers a full academic curriculum as well as courses related to aviation and the air transport industry. In language courses, an aviation vocabulary is integrated into regular lessons whenever appropriate. For example, in a language unit on food, students might simulate a dialogue between a steward and passengers who are having an on-board meal. To give students in language classes a firsthand look at the target language being used in the world of work, students also visit the Air France and Iberian Airline terminals at Kennedy Airport.

Other Teaching Strategies

As teachers of foreign languages begin to work into a program that encompasses career education in their classrooms, they should consider participating in any work experience or job placement program that their schools offer. They can work along with vocational education placement teachers or with guidance counselors in helping to place students who have had a second language in a job or in an internship of some kind, whether paid or unpaid. Practice in the target language in such placements will greatly help students build language skills and learn for themselves about the many community areas where there are jobs that are best served by a person with a second language.

To help students forge links with jobs, the foreign language teacher might also prepare a small classroom unit on job applications, résumés, and job interviews which will give students practice in emphasizing their skills in a target language. Employers who find it useful to have workers with second language skills should know that these students have the sought-after skills, and the students must learn to give these skills a prominent mention when seeking employment.

As students proceed through the language learning sequence, the teacher should continue to emphasize how the study of language, as conceived in a liberal arts sense, results in some practical skills that will enable students to function in particular occupations. Because students will be looking more and more upon job options in terms of personal choices, the need for individualized preparation becomes greater.

At the Live Oak High School in Morgan Hill, California, instructor Gerald Logan individualizes language study by offering his German students career education in six general areas: secretarial, stewardess, commercial employment, restaurant and motel work, scientific German, and home economics. Each student selects one of these areas and works out a semester contract with the teacher involving eighty hours of work. Using an extensive collection of materials which Logan has amassed, the student builds a project which will use foreign language skills as well as related skills. One student, who was interested in home economics, used information in the German magazines, *Neue Mode, Brigitte*, and *Schöner Wohnen*, to make clothing. She read articles in these magazines on clothing, then selected some fashions from *Neue Mode* for detailed study, mastered directions in German for making several dresses and blouses, and used German patterns. During her home economics period, the student, with help from the teacher, made the clothes. She received a semester of credit in German and a semester of credit in home economics for her 160 hours of work in both departments on this project.

In Dade County, Florida, a Title III grant program fostered the development of a highly individualized language program that was geared to career interests of students. The materials prepared for this program cover five vocational areas: automotive services, barber and beauty shop work, food services, radio and television repair, and retail sales. Students instruct themselves with packages in which there are tapes, visual materials, and printed materials. Teachers who use this program get special in-service training. The materials are intended to serve students from the ninth grade through adult education.

Another approach is to give students a list of the various kinds of occupations in each of the work clusters that have been designated by the U.S. Office of Education and ask them to decide which jobs specifically require proficiency in a second language. This can be followed up by a student compilation of tasks that must be performed by a person holding one of these jobs. Now the student has enough information to write a dialogue or monologue in the target language, incorporating characteristic situations on the job. The written material becomes a composition exercise to be corrected by the teacher. Next, the student makes an oral presentation to the class. The teacher's evaluation of student proficiency takes into account mastery of the tasks necessary in the job as well as command of vocabulary, grammatical structure, and pronunciation.

As students begin to narrow their fields of interest and competence, further specialization is possible. At this time, questions are likely to come up that the teacher and a general resource person may not be able to answer. This will require personal contacts with people in the specific occupations. To disseminate information gleaned in these contacts, these procedures might be useful:

(1) Interview, on audio or videotape, persons in various fields who actively use foreign languages in the course of their work: engineers, secretaries, hospital personnel, construction workers, mechanics, hotel clerks, and airline personnel.

(2) Interview native speakers about their culture with regard to specific topics in the world of work. Write a paper on the interview for presentation to the foreign language class and for publication in the school newspaper or news bulletin.

Often, teachers will find that students who enter foreign language classes already have specific and fairly well-developed skills that can be related from the outset to jobs in which knowledge of a second language is an asset. In such cases, the teacher's main task will be to evaluate the skills that students have learned in these corollary subject areas and relate them to foreign language study. For example, those with clerical skills might well enhance their opportunities for good jobs and advancement if they have competence in a foreign language.

Teachers should not postpone offering career-oriented instruction simply because few materials may have been published for a foreign language program with a career education focus. Start with materials at hand, and find ways to use them in the classroom. Materials needs should be discussed with sales representatives of publishing companies so that they will reconsider their textbook goals and develop appropriate materials. Meanwhile, an enthusiastic teacher probably will find that students are willing to share the responsibility for locating resources as part of their learning experience. Activities in which students discover relationships for themselves and learn to do other independent work are, after all, an important part of education.

Career emphasis implies a new focus, some redirection in the classroom, and greater integration with other disciplines. Therefore the foreign language teacher must reevaluate traditional components of the language course and decide which terms are essential in meeting new goals. At times it may be necessary to stress functional objectives at the expense of some traditional topics. Fortunately, the current emphasis being given in foreign language instruction to the teaching of literature and culture as a way of life allows for a here-and-now approach, and it is well suited to the purposes of career education. Using this approach, the foreign language teacher can answer more adequately the questions that have been raised by many students: "Why am I studying a *foreign* language?" and "Where am I going to use my knowledge of a foreign language?"

To be most effective in developing career education as a component of foreign language instruction, teachers must keep in close contact with guidance and administrative personnel in the school. Sometimes, poor communication results in the guidance counselor's directing all but the best students away from foreign language study. Counselors, as well as school administrators, must be fully aware of the philosophy of the foreign language educator and how it is to be implemented. Furthermore, they must see the results of success with many different students in terms of student enthusiasm, lowered attrition rates, and good parental response.

The elitist image of foreign language education will be eliminated only as foreign language teachers concentrate and coordinate their efforts by (1) providing foreign language curricular options that serve the entire school population, and (2) informing all sectors of the school and community of the goals and purposes of foreign language education.

Selected References

Born, Warren C. Editor. "Toward Student-Centered Foreign Language Problems." Report of the Working Committee of the 1974 Northeast Conference on the Teaching of Foreign Languages. New York, 1974.

Brod, Richard I. "Nonacademic Vocational Opportunities in Foreign Languages." ADFL Bulletin No. 3. New York: Association of Departments of Foreign Language. 1973.

Carney, Helen. "Developing a Dialogue about Careers with Employers." *Accent on ACTFL* (September-November 1974), vol. 4, no. v.

Cincinnati Public Schools. "Exploring Careers in International Travel, Trade, and Communications." Cincinnati, Ohio: Cincinnati Public Schools. 1974.

Ford, James F. "A Foreign Language Educator Looks at Career Education." *Arkansas Foreign Language Newsletter* (1973), vol. 7, no. ii.

Froning, Dorothy. "Vocational Opportunities for the Foreign Language Major." *Wichita State University Foreign Language Summary* (1971), vol. 6, no. ii.

Johns, H. H., Jr. "Career Development Becomes Foreign Language Objective." *Accent on ACTFL* (1972), vol. 3, no. i.

Keesee, Elizabeth. "Vocational Opportunities." *Hispania* (1972), vol. 55.

Lester, Kenneth A.; and Tamarkin, Toby. "Career Education." In volume 5 of *Responding to New Realities: ACTFL Review of Foreign Language Education*. Edited by Gilbert A. Jarvis. Skokie, Illinois: National Textbook. 1974.

Madison Public Schools. "Foreign Language: Key to Career Development." Madison, Wisconsin: Madison Public Schools. 1972.

Marottoli, Vincent. "The Success of Private Language Schools: A Lesson to Be Learned." *Foreign Language Annals* (1973), vol. 6.

Petrello, George J.; and Petrello, Barbara. "Help Wanted: Vocational Training for the Bilingual Job Market." *Business Education Forum* (1973), vol. 27, no. iv.

Prol, J. *Occupational Opportunities through Learning Foreign Languages*. Largo, Maryland: Prince George's Community College. 1973.

"Survey of Foreign Language Skills in Business and Service Organizations." ADFL Bulletin No. 5. New York: Association of Departments of Foreign Language. 1973.

Tinsley, Royal L., Jr. "Guidelines for College and University Programs in Translator Training." ADFL Bulletin No. 4. New York: Association of Departments of Foreign Language. 1973.

U.S. Department of Labor. *Foreign Languages and Your Career*. Washington, D.C.: U.S. Department of Labor. 1972.

U.S. Information Service. *Careers in Cross-Cultural Communication*. Washington, D.C.: U.S. Information Agency.

Walser, F. LeRoy. "A Preliminary Look at Potential Job Alternatives for Bilingual Students and Students of Foreign Languages: A Career Education Concept." ADFL Bulletin No. 4. New York: Association of Departments of Foreign Language. 1973.

8
Career Education in Health Sciences, Recreation, and Physical Education

American Alliance for Health, Physical Education, and Recreation

Gordon Jeppson
Program Administrator
Washington, D.C.

Hally Beth Poindexter
University of Houston
Houston, Texas

William J. Penny
East Stroudsburg State College
East Stroudsburg, Pennsylvania

Paul M. Hillar
Stanislaus County Department of Education
Modesto, California

Phyllis Ensor
Reisterstown, Maryland

8
Career Education in the Health Sciences and Recreation Classroom

The day is past when the physical education specialist served as the school health educator, first-aid specialist, athletic trainer, coach, recreation director, and teacher of all sports, games, and dance. Health, physical education, and recreation are recognized today as separate disciplines, and the professionals, because of their training, are becoming specialists who serve the needs of people of all ages.

The evolution from the umbrella concept, which once included a wide array of functions under the term "physical education," is reflected in the reorganization of the national professional association, the American Alliance for Health, Physical Education, and Recreation. This body now has national associations serving each of the disciplines — health educators by the Association for the Advancement of Health Education; recreation specialists by the American Association for Leisure and Recreation; and physical educators and sports educators by the National Dance Association, the National Association for Girls and Women in Sport, and the National Association for Sport and Physical Education. Outside the Alliance, there are other professional associations serving educators in these fields, among them the American School

Health Association, the School Health Division of the American Public Health Association, the National Recreation and Park Association, the National College Physical Education Association for Men, and the National Association of Physical Education for College Women.

Despite differences in professional preparation and the ways in which each discipline serves, there are many things in common and many close relationships. All of the disciplines deal specifically with the human factors involved in movement, well-being, and improving the quality of personal life. Because these interdisciplinary relationships sometimes confuse professionals and lay persons alike as to the distinctive functions of each discipline, it may be helpful to say what these are.

Physical education is concerned with human movement that develops neuromuscular skills, physical fitness, and an appreciation of bodily needs for physical development and exercise. It covers such interests as the dance (which also has esthetic origins), athletics of all kinds, and planned exercise programs to maintain good health or to restore health to persons with medical problems.

Health education in schools has three components: health instruction, health services, and the promotion of healthful school living. In all components, a major function is to translate scientific and medical information into layman's language in order to promote optimum health and to improve the quality of people's lives. Once, the primary concern in this discipline was the prevention and control of disease. Modern life has changed this emphasis, and today health education is focused on a far wider area — all of the physical, emotional, and even spiritual problems that confront humankind in its natural environment or which some persons have created for themselves.

Recreation as a discipline is moving toward use of the term "leisure" to describe its functions and to define its field. "Recreation" is a more limited term, because it implies a specific experience that an individual selects to meet personal needs or desires. The term "leisure" introduces an awareness of a long span of time — that large portion of human life in which people can make choices of the ways in which they use nonworking hours to enrich and broaden themselves and attain personal fulfillment.

Linkages with Career Education

Historically, career concerns have been an integral part of education in health, physical education, and recreation. Students have generally been attracted to these fields for two reasons: because they found great pleasure in them, and because they saw the potential for a career. Those interested in careers usually wanted to become health and physical education teachers, coaches, recreation leaders, or professional performers.

Students still are attracted to health, physical education, and recreation programs for the enjoyment they offer and for career reasons, but there are important changes. Increasingly, the focus in these programs is on improving the quality of life for all students, not just those who are the most highly skilled. Physical education, for example, now offers many individual and dual sport activities — such as tennis, golf, archery, bowling, and cross-country skiing — as well as team sports. Moreover, the career possibilities for students with health, physical education, and recreation knowledge have greatly expanded. The kinds of jobs available in the health field, for example, have proliferated. The increasing complexity of life has escalated demands for relief in the form of physical education and recreation services.

These changes have opened promising areas for career education in the three disciplines. There are many important ways in which career education can continue to broaden the appeal of health, physical education, and recreation subjects and link subject content to the growing awareness by students of personal needs throughout their lives. First, there is the fact that good mental and physical health, knowledge of bodily functions, and wise use of leisure have much to do with career success. In addition, the three disciplines now offer a wide variety of direct and indirect routes into future careers. Each discipline has its own career education potential, and it is therefore discussed separately.

Career Options in Health

Health education, like other parts of the education system, should seek opportunities to develop and reinforce the individual's self-image and feelings of self-worth. Those who lack positive self-concepts have little or no interest in futuristic goals such as careers, and certainly not in careers which demand a great deal of effort, time, and training cost.

Because any career choices that people make are influenced heavily by their value systems, some of the content in health education should help students examine their values as these relate to their future work, their future lives, their community, and their world. Do these values include the desire for economic independence, pride in accomplishment, and occupational satisfaction — and are these values supportive of good health? This is well worth examining, because it has been demonstrated repeatedly that students who can give correct answers in class to questions about risk-taking in such as drug use, venereal disease, smoking, and obesity still will use drugs, become obese, become infected with venereal disease, and smoke tobacco. It is a clear indication that knowledge alone does not guarantee positive life-enhancing behavior. Health education offers students many opportunities to develop, clarify, and periodically reassess these critical areas in career decision making and career success.

Health education must also give them an opportunity to examine their personal strengths and limitations in all aspects of emotional and physical health and the influence these factors may have on career choice. Obvious health considerations are physical disabilities, such as blindness, deafness, and bodily abnormality.

But it is not only what a person brings to a career that is important; equally important is what a career may do to that person. For this reason, a health education course should also encourage students to consider the influence that different careers might have on their health in terms of years of hard physical labor or years of sedentary work. Information on the stress associated with various careers should be included. Physicians indicate that a great number of illnesses have some psychosomatic origins and that the emotional response to the stress of daily activities often results in physical problems — headaches, ulcers, heart attacks, and emotional breakdowns. Another example of the impact that work may have on the individual is the heavy use of alcohol in certain occupations.

Indeed, occupational drinking patterns should be included in the information students seek when making career decisions.

Health education must also deal with the unexpected. No one expects an accident to happen, yet large numbers of people are disabled each year from automobile, home, and work-related accidents. This may force an individual to make a new career decision — one that makes allowances for disability, a particularly painful experience when one's work is dependent upon a specific physical skill. The loss of a hand or an arm may mean that even with a prosthesis, one can no longer perform the physical tasks of a well-established career. Physical disability resulting from a chronic disease may also force an alternative career decision. For example, a radio announcer who develops throat cancer and has a laryngotomy will no longer be able to perform in the same capacity. His whole personality and life-style may have been built round his radio voice.

Societal attitudes toward illness and toward any unusual features of a rehabilitation or recovery period may influence an individual's opportunity to choose a career. Often this is an acute problem for persons who have suffered an emotional breakdown, a problem from which no one is immune. With mood stabilizing drugs and antidepressants, recovery may be swift, and reentry into normal life, including return to work, may occur within a few weeks. Yet because of society's attitudes toward "the mental patient," an individual may be limited arbitrarily as a worker.

At each stage of life, there may be new limitations as a result of the continuing process of physical aging. But there may be new options as well. Knowing the role that good physical and mental health play as one grows older may motivate students to maintain health so that future choices will not be limited.

For young women, knowledge about health may mean making immediate decisions on family planning as well as career planning. Knowing more about pregnancy will help them realize that there is an optimum period for childbearing and that there may be a "too early" or "too late" time to have a family. Consideration of the advantages and disadvantages of early or late childbearing may well enter into decisions young women make about the timing and nature of their future careers.

Expanding Careers in Health

The public's growing awareness of health problems and view of health care as a right, rather than a privilege, have increased the demands and expectations for health services. People have been educated to use preventive health measures such as regular immunizations, Pap smears, family planning, dental checkups, eye examinations, multiphasic screening, and health maintenance checkups. These increased demands, combined with technological advances in health services, have created an array of new career opportunities. Some require years of prolonged training; others take a year or less of training; and still others require short-term, on-the-job training. These new careers cover an enormous range, from those that are in direct contact with patients to supportive services such as laboratory work, medical supplies and equipment sales, administration, advertising, and public relations.

The health care industry now employs more than 3.8 million persons, ten times the total in 1900. At the turn of the century, three out of five health workers were physicians. Today only one in ten health workers is a physician because new allied careers have extended the role of the physician, now at the top of a large pyramid of workers who have taken over many functions that only doctors and nurses were allowed to perform in years past. There are now more than 200 health careers listed by the National Health Council in its health careers directory. These careers provide not only a way to earn a living, but personal rewards from knowing that one's contribution is in some way — directly or indirectly — made to people who are in need of help. Such careers can offer great rewards to young people who are searching for meaning and personal satisfaction in their work.

Most people think of the traditional roles of doctor, dentist, and nurse when they think of health careers. Teachers should encourage students to investigate the entire range of health opportunities. They should give students a chance to visit and talk to allied health professionals during career days or on field trips so that students can learn for themselves that there are many health careers other than those most familiar to them. They should learn that there now is a great world of career opportunities in health.

Among the careers that may need to be brought to the attention of students are those of medical engineering or electronic specialist who design, operate, or maintain medical tools such as pacemakers, surgical equipment, life-support equipment, automatic monitoring electrocardiograms and other monitoring equipment, and automatic multitesting laboratory equipment. Many of these careers call for mechanical and engineering interests and abilities, but youth with such interests often are not aware of these careers as good possibilities for themselves. Students should also learn that today more women are becoming doctors and more men are becoming nurses. Moreover, the nurse's role has changed from doctor's helper to specialized roles such as nurse administrator, nurse practitioner, nurse associate, and nurse midwife. Each has its own defined area of responsibility, role, and function.

Exploring Health Careers

Students can learn firsthand about health careers through school and health fairs to which health workers of many kinds are invited to discuss and demonstrate their skills. Employment after school or during the summer in a doctor's office, dentist's office, hospital, or other health facility can greatly expand a student's knowledge of the importance and range of health occupations.

Field trips, when they are planned round specific learning objectives and do not attempt to serve too many students at one time, can also provide a rich firsthand experience for gleaning information on health careers. Possible sites for field trips include:

(1) Medical research center

(2) Public health department

(3) Physician's office

(4) Dentist's office

(5) Water treatment plant

(6) Refuse disposal and sewage treatment plant

(7) Industrial safety office

(8) Satellite or outreach health center

(9) Emergency information and referral center

(10) Emergency medical transportation center

(11) Prosthetic limb manufacture and fitting center

(12) Military hospital

(13) Civilian hospital

(14) Private medical clinic

(15) Mental health center

(16) Voluntary health agency

(17) Nurses' training school

(18) School nurse's office

(19) Consumer protection office

(20) University eye bank (or kidney bank, and so forth) facilities

Field trips can easily become exhausting for the teacher and unproductive for students unless good plans are made well in advance with the firm or industry to be visited and with students who are going on the field trip. Once at the work site, students must seize every opportunity to survey the jobs and assess them in terms of their difficulty, the skills required, the academic preparation needed, the nature of the work site, and the salary (optional) and job satisfactions inherent in the occupations.

For example, in a study of industrial safety, students might visit a number of sites and compare the kinds of jobs in the safety field and any different requirements from one firm to another. In addition, they might visit industrial sites where the nature of the work is such that many hazards would be present if it were not for safety equipment on the machinery and if workers had not been trained in prevention of unsafe practices, such as leaving tools lying about, failure to use hard hats or protective glasses, and the like. On a walk through an industrial plant, the teacher might point out potential hazards or might solicit student ideas about such hazards. Studies of industrial safety should also include learning about the requirements and enforcement of laws and ordinances that set occupational safety standards. Among sources of information for these studies are the Occupational Safety and Health Administration in the U.S. Department of Labor, the Bureau of Mines in the U.S. Department of the Interior, and state departments of health and labor.

In a study of medical laboratory services, students might visit an optical laboratory where lenses for eyeglasses are made, a dental laboratory, and a laboratory specializing in prostheses. These visits offer not only an in-depth view of each work site, but also an opportunity to compare tasks at each site and to determine the relative degrees to which artistic skills, engineering skills, knowledge of anatomy, and other factors are necessary.

Each unit of health education — health instruction, health services, and the promotion of healthful school living — also offers special opportunities for career development.

Health Instruction

The entire health instruction curriculum is based on research and the daily experience of hundreds of different scientists, technicians, and practitioners. The curriculum is dynamic and one whose content is changing constantly as a result of new scientific discoveries and changing patterns of service delivery in the health industry. All of this mean that the health instructor has an excellent opportunity (as well as an obligation toward increasing the human resource pool in health occupations) to give students insights into the wide variety of careers open to them. For example, in a single unit such as that on the heart and cardiovascular system, the teacher can heighten student interest in the studies by discussing a host of career options. In the study of anatomy and physiology of the cardiovascular system, some of the discussion might center on the functions of the following occupations in this field:

Physiologist

Exercise physiologist (stress testing)

Lab technician

Cine photographer

Hematologist

Electrocardiogram technician

Medical illustrator

Still photographer

In the unit study of heart disease, these occupations might also be discussed in some detail:

Physician, general practice

Physician, internist

Physician, anesthesiologist

Nurse, intensive coronary care unit

Nurse, operating room

Nurse, mobile emergency coronary care unit

Nurse's aide

Psychologist/psychiatrist

Pharmacist

Medical electronics engineer

Air ambulance pilot, helicopter

Health educator, patient education

Physician, cardiologist

Physician, vascular surgeon

Physician, cardiac surgeon

Nurse, general duty registered nurse

Nurse, emergency ward

Paramedic, mobile emergency coronary care unit

Ambulance driver

Radiologist

Hospital administrator

Heart-lung machine operator

Pharmacologist

Medical insurance agent

Consumer protection agent

Hospital orderly

Health Services

Teachers should also consider the career learning opportunities that are inherent in such school health services as screenings, immunization, and physical examinations. Merely explaining to students that they are "getting shots" to protect them against germs fails to present a total concept of public health programs and career opportunities.

First of all, in the school health clinic, students can gain personal information that is important in their consideration of career possibilities. During vision and hearing screening, for example, a student can learn about any sight or hearing limitations that might make it inadvisable to enter certain fields (findings of this kind should of course be verified by a physician). Sensitivity to immunizations given at school may also have implications for career planning.

Interest in health careers can be stimulated by telling students about all of the tasks involved in planning and carrying out immunization or screening programs. This will increase their awareness of the range of possibilities in health and of the fact that there are health specialists in public information and in the mass communications media as well as in program planning, health administration, public health nursing, and other more traditional roles.

Contacts with the school nurse, physician, psychologist, and health counselor may lead a student to become interested in these fields as a career. To build on this interest, teachers might ask students to serve as volunteer assistants to each of the health professionals. The student assistants might run information campaigns, keep records, or work as school health room receptionists.

When students see first aid being given in a serious emergency situation, teachers and counselors might build career interest in civilian or military emergency care occupations. In the civilian sector, there are likely to be many new job opportunities in this field as a result of the 1973 Emergency Medical Services Systems Act, which authorizes federal grants to help in the development of comprehensive emergency medical systems across the nation. It provides a wide array of career opportunities, such as helicopter medic, communications specialist, burn care technician, and area trauma care coordinator. School activities dealing with emergency care and other health care services should include related functions of the local fire and police departments, as well as those of community leaders and agency personnel who are involved with legislation, training, and administration in the health field.

Healthful School Living

One of the primary concerns of health education is the promotion of a safe and healthful school environment. In this area, career possibilities are numerous and far-ranging. Whether the school is a new one with the finest of facilities, or an old school with lighting or other structural problems, students can explore the contributions that have been made — or should be made — to their environment by architects, sanitary engineers, sanitation inspectors, electrical wiring inspectors, maintenance workers, and grounds supervisors. They might also examine the school setting, decide whether there is noise or air pollution in this setting, and learn what city planners can do to help prevent or overcome such problems.

If the school has problems involving the security of persons and property, students might examine these problems in the light of architectural design — the size and shape of school buildings in relation to their functions, and the kinds of internal communications and security systems that are present in the buildings. Careers in law enforcement could also be explored in connection with school security problems. School exercises in disaster preparedness might be used as a starting point for learning about careers in fire services, law enforcement, radiological monitoring, radio communications, and the like.

Students may become interested in careers through school food services, including management, purchasing, nutrition, menu planning, and the storage, processing, preparation, and distribution of food. A school health instructor can team nutrition learning with career education by presenting a problem-solving lesson to help students understand these various facets of food service. If the cafeteria happens to be one that resembles a battlefield, with food used as ammunition, or if there are boycotts of the lunch line because students complain about the food, the problem solving might focus on this. Students could examine the tasks of each food service worker, the pay, and any career ladder opportunities — or lack of them — in the food service field. If students are dissatisfied with the food they are offered, they might give special attention to the tasks in menu selection, food purchase, and food preparation in terms of the persons who are most responsible for each of these elements. Then, on the basis of their research, students might propose feasible changes to improve the school lunch menu or the lunchroom atmosphere.

Career Options in Physical Education

Traditionally, physical education in secondary schools has been geared toward development of sports skills and physical fitness. Only too often, performance standards have been imposed externally without recognition of an individual's personal motivations and aspirations. While external performance standards do motivate some students, they cause others to withdraw from experiencing their own individual levels of excellence. Whenever this has been the case, it has produced some bitter fruit. An article in the New York *Times* described the point of view of a person not highly talented in sports but who becomes a nonparticipant:

> SportsWorld is a state of mind in which the winner becomes good because he won; the loser, if not actually bad, is at least reduced, and must prove himself over again, through competitition....But for most Americans, the specialness of sport, the joyous, yes ennobling quality that can lift us out of our lives toward new standards of excellence, that can inspire us to stretch our bodies and spirits, will still be out of reach....American sports will still emphasize highly structured contests for the talented elite, and most Americans will still be discarded by so-called physical education teachers, by recreation supervisors, and by coaches, discarded to stand along gymnasium walls and cheer for others, discarded to watch forever from the stands or in front of the television set.

Awareness of this problem, and the desire to serve all students well, is bringing change into physical education in our secondary schools. The trend is toward enriching the curriculum with a variety of one- and two-person sports, and the adoption of a view of sport as many forms of movement rather than as a contest to be won or lost. Career education has an important place in this changing environment because it emphasizes the need of all students for career development in all areas of school instruction, and it helps to make physical educators aware of the rich resources they have to offer every student who enters their classes.

Obviously, there still are certain career options related to movement where knowledge and adherence to external standards are essential for success. Anyone interested in pursuing a professional career in sports must measure personal performance levels against those needed by the professional athlete. However, many other people in many other occupations also benefit from participation in some sport, dance, or other form of exercise. Movement serves to fulfill the societal needs of man by providing relief from other pursuits and by offering a universal language and common point of communication.

The more complex and industrial a society becomes, and the more remote the physical demands on the individual, the more crucial and supportive the role of physical activity becomes. The increasingly sedentary life-style by a large part of our population often is attended by emotional and mental strain. Thus voluntary and planned involvement in movement activities becomes an essential ingredient in maintaining a balance in one's life.

Students' career education needs in relation to physical education cover a range as broad as that displayed in individual skills performance. Those who excel in selected skills may enter the ranks of professionals, while others can use their knowledge of movement in various forms of teaching, in allied areas, in other fields requiring physical prowess, and in careers where there is need to get some physical release or to maintain physical vitality, such as occupations that may lead to intellectual stress (scholar, researcher, accountant), and occupations involving minute or taxing physical skills (dentistry, drafting, secretarial, assembly line, and production work).

The development of career awareness across this span of student interests does not require the displacement of physical education subject matter. Rather, career education is largely a matter of focus, and it enriches course content and increases student interest by helping all students discover personal rewards that they can carry away from their physical education classes.

Students with Peripheral Interests

For those whose interest is faint in physical education for its own sake, or in physical education and allied careers, the teacher could encourage an exploration of the many relationships between occupational demands in careers that interest the students and some of the underlying concepts in physical education — the development of dependability, accuracy, timeliness, communication, and motor skills. For example, young people who are eager to become doctors, engineers, electricians, or artists could learn the importance of needs for fine motor skills in these occupations and how such skills can be cultivated in physical exercise and games.

Another area that might be explored is the degree of physical demand in various types of work. In the *Dictionary of Occupational Titles*, the U.S. Department of Labor includes in its occupational analyses the degree of physical demand usually required — sedentary, light, medium, heavy, and very heavy — that are requisite in activities such as carrying, lifting, pushing, and pulling. Students might check this dictionary for physical demands and other content in occupations that interest them and add it to whatever else they have learned about the occupation. Then they might analyze what can be learned in the physical education program. They are likely to discover that even if they are not preparing for a physical education career, they are preparing in physical education classes for careers that they find interesting and potentially satisfying. Through career education approaches of this kind, the physical education teacher has an opportunity not only to motivate student interest in the physical education program, but to contribute to the fund of realistic, factual knowledge that students possess as they get ready to make important occupational decisions.

Students Seeking Related Careers

At the opposite end of the spectrum in terms of student interest in physical education are the young people who seek a career in physical education or a related field. This group of students also needs time in the classroom to learn about the underlying concepts of physical education. It is imperative that these students understand not only the outcome of movement in the form of a skill, but also learn about the structure of the body as it applies to the end product. The concepts of biomechanics, exercise physiology, muscular kinesiology, and motor learning should be an integral part of the curriculum. By spending a portion of the time now available for teaching physical education on concept development, teachers will provide students with a basis for applying knowledge about movement to various career options, including those that do not involve movement per se but require an understanding of movement.

Athletics and Sports Careers

Competitive athletic programs in schools, colleges, and professional ranks demand talent on the playing fields as well as knowledgeable coaches, athletic administrators, team managers, and athletic trainers. Many young men and women have been attracted to a career in athletics as a result of high school sports participation. Some have risen to financial security and levels of national admiration because of their athletic ability. Not all professional players are outstanding performers, however, and those who achieve high performance levels may have relatively short careers. But their advanced knowledge of certain skills often opens other career options to them. Among these occupational options are athletic coach, athletic administrator, and team manager.

The athletic coach uses his knowledge of training, sports skills, and strategies in working with talented persons who seek superior professional levels of skill performance. Coaching opportunities range from the Little League level to the heights of Olympic and various national championships levels. At all levels there is an opportunity for a major role in the success of individual players and teams.

Students learn much about coaching as sports participants, but their experiences can be broadened through directed readings and planned observations of coaching techniques and behavior if they visit training camps and practice sessions and participate in coaching clinics, have conversations with successful coaches and athletes, and watch a film review of a game.

Certification of secondary school athletic coaches seems imminent. Such certification will be based on scientific collegiate preparation and practical experience, but it will still keep the secondary school coaching field open to people whose major field of training has been in academic disciplines other than physical education and sports. The purpose of certification is to assure competent coaching techniques while protecting the health and safety of student participants.

Athletic administrative positions are part of both educational and professional sports. The administrator's tasks include scheduling athletic events, planning tournaments and transportation, making insurance arrangements, planning the use of facilities, lining up game officials, purchasing equipment and uniforms, developing and maintaining relationships with sports organizations, serving as the official voice for the athletic program, and finding sources of finance for athletics. Skills for this occupation frequently are acquired during experience as a player, coaching assistant, or student team manager.

The team manager in some ways is like an administrative intern. The job calls for supervision of laundry facilities, inventories, and repair of equipment and uniforms. Daily preparation for practices, scrimmage, roadtrips, and competitive play keeps the team manager in close touch with administrative requirements of the team and offers invaluable experience for moving up the administrative ladder.

Athletic trainers also perform vital sports functions. Somewhat comparable to coaches, they supervise the preparation of wrestlers for matches and the training of long-distance runners and other single competitors in sports. In the past, most athletic trainers got their experience as interns to a respected trainer; but in recent years, this occupation has become a significant part of high school athletic programs, and many young people now begin learning the occupation through volunteer work in the high school training room. In addition, there are clinics and other training experiences offered to interested high school students by companies that sell athletic equipment and medical supplies. Later, high school graduates can continue in this field as student trainers in college and — with additional preparation in the field of physical therapy — can gain certification as athletic trainers. Those who do not eventually become professional trainers often discover viable careers in physical therapy and related work in hospitals and private practice.

Careers in Teaching

Students interested in teaching physical education soon discover that there are various skill levels at which they can teach. If they want to become a college or public school teacher, they will in all likelihood need formal college preparation. On the other hand, there are positions as teachers' aides and teaching posts in adult education — for example, the YMCA and community centers — which require less formal preparation. Whatever the job, teaching physical activities requires understanding the structure and function of the body as it relates to movement forms, the learner, and the teaching-learning process.

A physical education teacher can encourage students to enter this field through a planned program of observation and assistance. Experience in high school as a gymnasium supervisor, intramural assistant, equipment manager, or leader of a sports club or other student group can help students learn one important component of teaching — how to organize and handle administrative duties. Other ways to help students explore the nature of the occupation is to give them responsibility for locker room supervision, roll checks, equipment issue, facility safety checks, instructional assistance, and athletic team management. Not only do students greatly benefit from these career exploration experiences, teachers get interested helpers and feedback on their program from students who have seen it from many different angles.

Students considering careers as physical education teachers will find that they can widen their horizons on careers still further by observing physical educators at various sites, such as other schools, private clubs, and civic centers. Professional teachers of sports and athletics include tennis, golf, archery, and swimming instructors at resorts, hotels, health and exercise clubs, swimming centers, and camps. Discussions with many different "on-line" practitioners, participation as volunteer workers in different programs, and employment after school or in the summer can further expand the students' knowledge of what it's like to be a physical education instructor.

Through these varied contacts, they will also learn that teaching opens the door to other professional opportunities. Among these career possibilities are jobs as writers of instructional materials, researchers in various areas concerned with physiological and psychological aspects of human performance, and owners and managers of clubs and other sports-oriented establishments.

Allied Career Options

A great number of allied career areas develop from interests in physical education and sports, ranging from occupations that have direct and obvious connections to those with more subtle connections. The design, production, and sales of sports equipment and the design and improvement of facilities for many different sports are fields open to persons with physical education and athletic interests. Moreover, the demand is brisk in certain sectors. Industry seeks designs for more durable badminton racquets, more protective football helmets, and safer equipment. Women athletes have been instrumental in opening new jobs in the design of tennis, golf, and ski apparel that is both attractive and functional.

Interest in physical activity has encouraged expanded building programs for school, college, agency, community, and governmental facilities for athletics and sports, and has opened many new jobs for the sports professional. Working with architects and engineers, the sports expert can contribute to the development of functional and safe facilities. Many professional golf instructors now are golf course architects, able skiers manage and develop ski resorts, and a great many athletic coaches serve as consultants to manufacturers of artificial turf and other playing surfaces. Some dancers no longer perform; they use their talents and experience in stage and set design. At the same time, directors of dance groups, choreographers, and artistic production specialists are being sought for high school and college programs in the performing arts.

The wide-ranging career interests of physical education students are stimulated in a variety of ways. Science classes may challenge them in their assessment of the physiological parameters of an individual when exercising. The physical education teacher may arrange visits to clinics and hospitals so that students can observe the exercise and physical rehabilitation of patients; and students may even become involved in the physical rehabilitation of someone in their own family — be it an inherent disability or a postoperative recuperation from surgery, or the healing of a broken bone or torn ligament. The extent to which students choose careers in physical education and related fields is a function of their desires and perceptions, plus the ability of the physical educator and other teachers to expand the perceptions of students and stimulate their interests.

Two extensive allied fields offer some specific examples of how the physical education teacher can use course content to build bridges between physical education and the fulfillment of students' occupational interests. These fields are sports medicine and sports communications.

Sports Medicine

The emerging field of sports medicine fascinates many young people. Using the expertise of physicians, physiologists, psychologists, engineers, physical educators, and electronic specialists, workers in this field are exploring many problems related to medical aspects of sports, games, and dance. Their functions range from rehabilitation of persons with sports injuries to prediction of human responses to the stresses of space exploration. To encourage student awareness and interest in sports medicine, the physical education teacher might encourage and help students get the following experiences during the secondary school years:

(1) Work as a class leader in an adaptive program for youngsters with physical limitations

(2) Visit therapy centers to observe the work and discuss the program with clinicians and their patients

(3) Plan and participate in a conditioning program in which physiological changes in weight, rest, regular heart rate, exercise heart rate, blood pressure, and other physio-

logical data are noted and recorded (could be done under the direction of the athletic trainer, school physician, or physical educator)

(4) Serve as a subject in the study of exercise stress at a nearby university or hospital

(5) Volunteer services at a hospital in an exercise stress laboratory or in a physical therapy unit

(6) Serve as a student assistant to the athletic trainer in the high school's athletic program

(7) Attend professional conferences on rehabilitation and sports therapy

(8) Elect high school courses focusing on human physiology and human health

Sports Communications

In the communications field, there is increasing interest in people who know sports and can communicate that knowledge in an interesting and informed way as newspaper reporters or as radio and television sportscasters. To stimulate student interest in these career fields, physical education teachers might do the following:

(1) Invite local reporters to class to talk about their profession, and schedule visits to the local newspaper, television, and radio stations (in many local communities, there are cable television stations which are committed to local coverage and might be willing to allow students to develop local programming)

(2) Let local newspapers, television, and radio stations know about students who are available for after-school work, and provide placement information to students

(3) Have brochures prepared which describe new aspects of school sports, dance, and related programs

(4) Provide bulletin boards, and make students responsible for keeping them current on information about class tournaments, interscholastic sports, and newspaper clippings

(5) Encourage accurate and able sports coverage in the school newspaper

(6) Encourage students to interview leading school athletes and send press releases to local newspapers

(7) Start a camera club, or provide photographic coverage of sports events by students, and set up an appropriate display area for photographs

(8) Get students to help keep scores and other interscholastic game statistics

(9) Give students a chance to have a leadership role in developing and selling advertising and putting together programs to hand out at sports events

(10) Let highly motivated students travel with coaches to scout other teams in order to learn coaching techniques and to enhance their understanding of interscholastic sports

(11) Get permission for a regular morning homeroom period of sports discussion or a lunch hour sports synopsis to be announced over the school's public address system

(12) Encourage students to work on the sports section of the school yearbook

(13) Get a news exchange going between schools in the same district or between sports rivals

These activities should not be limited to students whose major interest is physical education. By calling upon students whose chief interests are in other subjects to participate in these events, physical education teachers can widen the scope of their teaching and help make all students aware of their life-long needs for physical exercise and well-being.

Career Options in Recreation

There has been a massive surge in recent years in the field of discretionary time activities. Leisure and recreation now constitute a $150 billion industry that has great potential for continuing expansion. Contributing to this growth have been (1) increases in the population, especially in urban areas where the pace and the compression of people into limited space multiply the recreational needs, (2) greater mobility, (3) earlier retirement, (4) automation of work, (5) better education, accompanied by awareness of cultural resources and the importance of physical and mental fitness, (6) larger blocks of free time on holiday weekends, (7) shorter workweeks, and (8) changing value systems which place a higher premium on personal development and interpersonal relationships and a somewhat lower value on the traditional ethic of work for work's sake.

Occupational opportunities are broad in the field of leisure-time pursuits. A 1967 human resources study predicted that the 303,000 full-time jobs in parks and recreation at that time would climb to the equivalent of an estimated 1.2 million full-time positions by 1980, using both full- and part-time jobs to arrive at this total.

The National Recreation and Park Association has identified more than seven hundred kinds of occupations which call for knowledge and skills in the area of leisure-time activities. Some of them have other skills components, and some are new jobs that have not yet made their way into the Labor Department's *Dictionary of Occupational Titles.* The occupations are of an enormous variety because they are located in widely varying places. Among these are urban parks, wilderness areas, resorts, industrial and business sites, youth centers, commercial recreation enterprises, religious centers, retirement centers, hospitals, mental institutions, prisons, stadiums, community centers, zoos, acquariums, housing developments, environmental control and other agencies at all levels of government, and private clubs. The range of job opportunities runs from positions requiring less than a high school diploma to those requiring unique and highly specialized education. Many jobs can be filled by handicapped persons.

Although the rapid emergence of the leisure industry has made it hard to identify all of its potential employment opportunities, most of these fall under four occupational headings:

(1) *Recreation services:* Jobs that call for planning, creating, and supervising programs, and for providing leadership and instruction in recreational activities.

Careers in this field involve a large amount of personal interaction

(2) *Recreation resources:* Jobs that include those related to the planning, development, maintenance, and protection of natural and synthetic resources used for leisure purposes and the production, distribution, and sale of recreation products. These jobs form a support system for the recreation services group

(3) *Tourism:* Jobs that include publicizing tourist facilities; making travel arrangements for tourists; providing transportation, housing, food, and services for tourists; and offering activities for tourist participation

(4) *Amusement and entertainment:* Jobs that are centered round amusements such as skating rinks; live, filmed, or broadcast performances; athletic contests; instruction in entertainment skills; training of animals for entertainment purposes; and personal services in places of entertainment

A career education program for these occupations will greatly enhance a student's opportunities for entry-level employment during and after the high school years. However, it is highly unlikely that a single secondary school discipline can give adequate attention to a field so interdisciplinary in its content. Every teacher and counselor in the school should be a resource for career education in recreation and leisure occupations. The physical education teacher has much to offer in sports-oriented occupations. Art and music teachers can develop important leisure-linked knowledge and skills in their classrooms. The communicative arts — a significant element in a great many leisure and recreation jobs — are the specialties of English and foreign language teachers. Science teachers can play a major role in the career education of students who want to work in forests and other outdoor sites.

Teaching Models for Career Education

To facilitate the integration of career education for the leisure occupations into the school curriculum, the U.S. Office of Education–sponsored curriculum guidelines (Verhoven and Vinton, 1972) give specific classroom activities in mathematics, the language arts, the expressive arts, science, and social studies. The material covers the various career education levels — awareness, exploration, orientation, and skills development — and focuses on infusing career education into the various disciplines with no drastic changes required in the extant curriculum. In the following two models (adapted from the USOE publication), mathematics and the expressive arts are each linked with leisure for a look at some of the types of occupations that can be found in these fields. The interdisciplinary elements are strikingly obvious.

Model A — *Relating the fields of mathematics and leisure to careers*

This model contains four sample exercises wherein mathematics and leisure occupations are linked to specific jobs.

Sample Exercise 1 — Broadcast program assistant

The program assistant at a local television station is arranging rehearsal rooms for auditions being held for a new musical group to consist of five guitars and two drums. The musicians who show up are twelve guitarists and five drummers.

    a) How many combinations of guitar players can be chosen?

    b) How many combinations of drummers can be chosen?

    c) How many different sets of musicians can be chosen for the group?

    d) How many audition rooms will be needed?

Sample Exercise 2 — Roulette *tourneur* (dealer)

An American roulette wheel has 38 compartments round its rim. Two of these are numbered "0" and "00" and are colored green. Of the others numbers (1 through 36), half are colored red and half are black. In order for the roulette dealer to have control of the game, he or she needs to know the answers to the following questions:

    a) What is the probability of the ball landing on "7"?

    b) What is the probability that a black number will win?

    c) What is the probability of each of the following coming up:

        1) Any number from "1" to "12"?

2) Either "0" or "00"?

3) A red number?

4) A red number, if the previous 25 spins had resulted in a black number coming up?

5) A number that is not red?

Sample Exercise 3 — Billiards instructor

The billiards instructor wants to determine the path of the following billiard balls. Complete the path of each, assuming that the ball stops when it reaches a corner.

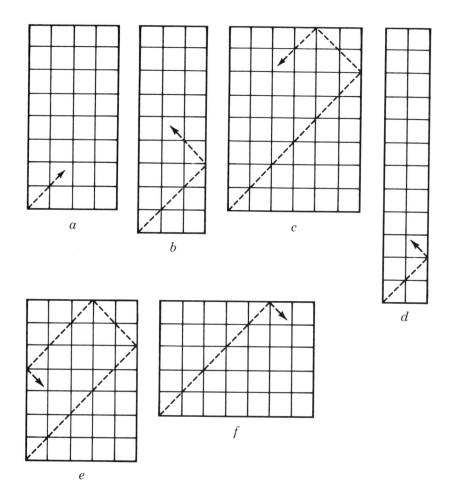

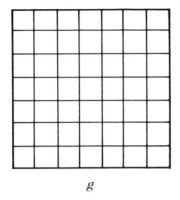

g

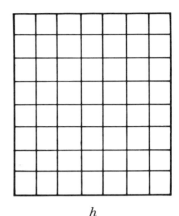

h

a) On which table does the ball have the simplest path? Can you explain why?

b) What do you notice about the paths of the balls on tables *e* and *f*? Can you explain?

c) Do you think the ball will always end up in a corner? (Use diagram *g*.)

d) If the ball starts from the lower left-hand corner, do you think that it can end up in any of the four corners? If so, why? If not, why? (Use diagram *h*.)

Sample Exercise 4 — Craps table overseer

The dots on a single die range from one to six; thus the numbers on a pair of dice can be added together to make from two ("snake eyes") to twelve ("boxcars"). In order for the table to "win for the house," the overseer needs to know the "odds." In other words, he or she must know the answers to such questions as the following:

a) What is the probability of throwing a double?

b) What is the probability of throwing a seven (two and five, six and one, or four and three)?

c) What is the probability that one die will have a number less than three and the other die will have a number greater than three?

d) What is the probability of throwing a ten? A twelve?

e) What is the probability of *not* throwing a double?

Model B — *Relating the fields of leisure and the expressive arts to careers*

Because children learn early in life from visual and tactile activities, the disciplines of the expressive arts — dance, drama, music, physical education, and athletics — are excellent vehicles for career education. When they are combined with an equally desirable discipline such as "leisure," the teacher has a sure-fire course that will attract many students.

The following sample exercise give the student an opportunity to develop awareness of self while exploring occupations that are linked with jobs in leisure-time pursuits. Although the arts are often segmented by teachers into grade level, true student progress is based upon the developmental levels of children and young adults, rather than their age and grade level.

Sample Exercise 1 — Dance

a) Awareness

1) Have the class observe and report on rhythms they have discovered outside the classroom (movement of trees, animals, and so forth), recognizing that each student is unique in his or her style of movement.

2) Have students associate rhythm and movements with mood (use music to create moods).

3) Have the students create interpretive movements for some area of study in leisure occupations — rain and wind, volcanoes erupting, a trip into the forest.

4) Conduct a folk dance festival with square dances, social dances, and so forth.

5) Have the students read about famous dance entertainers (ballet, tap, interpretive, and so on).

b) Exploration

1) Encourage long-range and cooperative projects related to leisure occupations.

2) Observe and discuss line, color, texture in relation to projects.

3) Have students make a scrapbook of travel brochures. Have them design such a brochure.

4) Have the students design an advertisement for a travel magazine or a theater performance.

5) Have students prepare for a sidewalk art show.

c) Orientation and skills development

1) Work separately with students who are interested in supportive roles for dance performers.

2) Encourage students to act as instructors of the dance.

3) Involve interested students in such things as costume design and making, set design and construction, makeup, and stage lighting.

4) Have students write critiques of performances they witnessed, plan programs that are similar to these performances, and perform other supportive roles for performances.

5) Have students serve as a booking agent for performing classmates.

6) Have students arrange programs for PTA, service clubs, and elementary schools.

Sample Exercise 2 — Drama

a) Awareness

1) Develop student self-awareness and self-confidence.

2) Encourage spontaneous, creative play.

3) Plan student pantomimes and creative dramatics.

4) Explain jobs and roles of supportive personnel.

5) Have students study how to write a play and then write one.

6) Make scrapbooks of lighting, stage sets, costuming, and so forth.

7) Attend theater performances, visit television studios.

8) Exchange dramatic presentations with other schools.

b) Exploration

1) Have students use role-playing monologues and dialogues.

2) Encourage both spontaneous creative dramatics and play writing.

3) Encourage improvement in style of oral and written critiques.

4) Help students learn the techniques of videotaping.

5) Have them make and edit a film of class performances.

6) Encourage them to observe work of supportive personnel in theaters — ushers, ticket takers, lighting crews, and so on.

7) Visit a booking agency so that students can learn the functions of this occupation.

c) Orientation and skills development

1) Encourage the reading of plays, operettas, and television scripts.

2) Have students write critiques of selected television dramas or live theater performances.

3) Use tape recordings so that students can improve their skills in pronunciation, enunciation, and interpretive reading.

4) Have students write scenarios, first outlining the plot.

5) Have students design a set, sketch costumes, or demonstrate character makeup.

6) Encourage them to work with the school publication to advertise performances and to publish critiques on dramatic productions.

7) Encourage students to participate in supportive roles for school productions on local tour.

Sample Exercise 3 — Music

a) Awareness

1) Help students establish a music center where they can explore sounds of instruments.

2) Have them create rhythms with instruments to illustrate circus animals walking.

3) Use singing rounds and conversational singing.

4) Have the class listen to different kinds of records and select the appropriate music to accompany a series of pictures or slides.

5) Take a field trip to a park or the zoo to make tape recordings of sounds. Have the class pinpoint any rhythmic passages.

6) Go to a concert or a band practice.

b) Exploration

1) Have the class listen to selected music for mood and then match the music to dance, art, or drama.

2) Have the students prepare a musical background for a dramatic presentation.

3) Invite soloists and group performers to the classroom.

4) Give concerts in elementary schools.

5) Visit a television studio to learn about the use of music in telecasts of various kinds.

6) Use excerpts of operettas, musicals, and familiar concert themes as often as possible.

7) Encourage students to compose simple melodies, and allow time for them to perform them.

8) Help students coordinate music for school dramas, dance, gymnastics, and art exhibits.

9) Play music from different cultures and encourage the students to prepare a musical travelogue.

10) Encourage students to visit — and even serve an internship in — recording studios, music stores, music libraries, and concert halls.

Summary

Implementation of career education in the health science and recreation occupations — as in all other career fields — needs the support of the community if it is to succeed. If school-age youth are to explore careers and develop skills that are pertinent to real-life situations, many barriers between the school and the community must be bridged by special efforts to inform the community and gain its support. Moreover, exploration of careers in these fields should be based, at least for a starting point, on local or regional needs and conditions. The access to information and jobs probably is better the nearer home those jobs happen to be.

Career education in recreation and leisure-time areas should not lose sight of the fact that it is important for all future adults to develop interests, skills, and awareness of the uses to which leisure time can be put. This is true whether students become homemakers, lawyers, or construction workers, or whether they enter some occupation outside the leisure field. Leisure is more than a host of occupations; it is a resource that all students should learn to use well, and it is the responsibility of the schools to prepare them to do so.

Selected References

American Association for Health, Physical Education, and Recreation. "Careers in Physical Education and Coaching for Boys." Washington, D.C.: American Association for Health, Physical Education, and Recreation.

_____. "It's time to Stop Talking about Women's Rights in Sports." Washington, D.C.: American Association for Health, Physical Education, and Recreation.

_____. "Your Future as a Teacher of Elementary School Physical Education." Washington, D.C.: American Association for Health, Physical Education, and Recreation.

Bayliss, Sylvia J.; *et al. Career Opportunities — Community Service and Related Specialists.* Chicago: J. G. Ferguson Publishing Company. 1970.

Journal of Health, Physical Education, and Recreation (September 1974).

McCall, Virginia; and McCall, Joseph R. *Your Career in Parks and Recreation.* New York: Julian Messner, Publishers, Inc. 1970.

National Recreation and Parks Association. "Publications on Parks, Recreation, and Leisure." Arlington, Virginia: National Recreation and Parks Association.

_____. "Service to Humanity: A Career in Parks, Recreation, and Leisure Services." Arlington, Virginia: National Recreation and Parks Association.

U.S. Department of Labor. *Dictionary of Occupational Titles.* Washington, D.C.: U.S. Government Printing Office. Various years.

Verhoven, Peter J.; and Vinton, Dennis A. "Career Education for Leisure Occupations: Curriculum Guidelines for Recreation, Hospitality, and Tourism." Lexington: University of Kentucky. December 1972.

Webster, William Douglas. *Recreation Leadership Training for Teenage Youth: A Study of Basic Program Development.* Eugene: Oregon University, Center for Leisure Study and Community Service. 1970.

Index

CAREER EDUCATION IN THE ACADEMIC CLASSROOM was composed in Century Schoolbook by Twin Typographers. Cover art was done by Linda Stevens, and mechanicals were prepared by Fran Clements of Bailey-Montague & Associates. The book was printed by Paragon Press and bound by Mountain States Bindery.